THE RIDDLE OF INTELLIGENCE

Explanations in the Social Sciences

Explanations in the Social Sciences are short, authoritative books written by global scholars for students and the general public. Each volume explores a single question often asked about the demands and challenges of being human from an historical, as well as contemporary perspective. This series is designed to demonstrate how S.T.E.M. education must include the social sciences if we are to deal successfully with the risks and uncertainties of life today and in the future.

Series Editors:
John Terrell, Field Museum of Natural History, Chicago
Mark L. Golitko, University of Notre Dame
Luis A. Muro Ynoñán, Field Museum of Natural History

Volume 2
The Riddle of Intelligence: It's Not What You Think
John Terrell, Eugene Anderson, Foreman Bandama, Abhik Ghosh, and Marcia Leenen-Young

Volume 1
Sex, Risk, and Society: When Is Sex Dangerous?
Sarah H. Pollock

THE RIDDLE OF INTELLIGENCE

It's Not What You Think

John Terrell, Eugene Anderson, Foreman Bandama,
Abhik Ghosh, and Marcia Leenen-Young

berghahn
NEW YORK • OXFORD
www.berghahnbooks.com

First published in 2025 by
Berghahn Books
www.berghahnbooks.com

© 2025, 2026 John Terrell, Eugene Anderson, Foreman Bandama,
Abhik Ghosh, and Marcia Leenen-Young
First paperback edition published in 2026

All rights reserved. Except for the quotation of short passages
for the purposes of criticism and review, no part of this book
may be reproduced in any form or by any means, electronic or
mechanical, including photocopying, recording, or any information
storage and retrieval system now known or to be invented,
without written permission of the publisher.

Library of Congress Cataloging-in-Publication Data

Names: Terrell, John, author.
Title: The riddle of intelligence : it's not what you think / John Terrell, Eugene
  Anderson, Foreman Bandama, Abhik Ghosh, and Marcia Leenen-Young.
Description: New York : Berghahn Books, 2025. | Series: Explanations in the
  social sciences ; volume 2 | Includes bibliographical references and index.
Identifiers: LCCN 2025002908 (print) | LCCN 2025002909 (ebook) |
  ISBN 9781805399940 (hardback) | ISBN 9781805399964 (epub) |
  ISBN 9781805399971 (adobe pdf)
Subjects: LCSH: Intellect.
Classification: LCC BF431 .T4218 2025 (print) | LCC BF431 (ebook) |
  DDC 153.9—dc23/eng/20250208
LC record available at https://lccn.loc.gov/2025002908
LC ebook record available at https://lccn.loc.gov/2025002909

British Library Cataloguing in Publication Data
A catalogue record for this book is available from the British Library

EU GPSR Authorized Representative
LOGOS EUROPE, 9 rue Nicolas Poussin, 17000, LA ROCHELLE, France
Email: Contact@logoseurope.eu

ISBN 978-1-80539-994-0 hardback
ISBN 978-1-83695-470-5 paperback
ISBN 978-1-80539-996-4 epub
ISBN 978-1-80539-997-1 web pdf

https://doi.org/10.3167/ 9781805399940

Contents

List of Illustrations   vi
Acknowledgments   xi

Introduction   1

Chapter 1. Basic Questions   21

Chapter 2. Possible Answers   41

Chapter 3. Intelligence Redefined   59

Conclusion: Being Intelligent   92

Reference List   115
Index   131

Illustrations

Figures

0.1. Normalized distribution of IQ on the Wechsler Adult Intelligence Scale (WAIS) with a mean of 100 and a standard deviation of 15. It is commonly assumed by many today that like a person's height and weight, their intelligence can be measured to discover how smart they are stacked up against other people. When charted as a normal distribution, approximately 68 percent of adults are believed to fall within one standard distribution above and below the mean. Dmcq, CC BY-SA 3.0, via Wikimedia Commons. xiv

0.2. Claudius Ptolemy, a Greek mathematician, astronomer, and geographer who lived in Alexandria in the second century AD. His mathematical arguments were so influential that the ancient Earth-centered view of the universe is known today as the Ptolemaic system. Picture from a sixteenth-century book frontispiece. Theodor de Bry, Public domain, via Wikimedia Commons. 5

0.3. The decisive role of prior assumptions. What we take for granted can play a decisive role, for example, in how we see our place in the Universe. Bottom row, left: Muhammad, CC BY-SA 3.0, via Wikimedia Commons; middle: Public domain, Wikimedia Commons; right: Arthur Berry (1862–1929), Public domain, Wikimedia Commons. © John Edward Terrell. 5

0.4. The down-draught iron smelting furnace near Kasungu, Malawi. The stack is made of baked clay taken from termite mounds and is sufficiently high to permit the furnace to attain smelting temperature by natural draft rather than with an air blast provided by pumping bellows. Source: David J. Killick, used with permission. 11

0.5. (top) Subway map—an example of *situational mapping*. London Underground geographic map, CC 3.0, via Wikimedia Commons. (bottom) Music notation—an example of *sequential mapping*—for "Mary Had a Little Lamb" based on a poem by Sarah Josepha Hale, 1823. Sarah Josepha Hale & Lowell Mason, Public domain, via Wikimedia Commons.   17

0.6. Can you tell whether the central square on the right is bigger than the one on the left? Hint: appearances can be deceiving. © John Edward Terrell.   19

1.1. (a) A Cartesian coordinate system on a two-dimensional plane defied by two perpendicular axes. Gustavb, GNU Free Documentation License, CC BY-SA 3.0, via Wikimedia Commons. (b) Ternary plot. Tobias1984, CC BY-SA 3.0, via Wikimedia Commons. 24

1.2. (a) Conventional everyday WHAT? or CATEGORICAL thinking is your brain's way of identifying what it may be dealing with in the world based on what it sees as the defining *traits, characteristics, elements, ingredients,* or *dimensions* (labeled here as X, Y, and Z) of what it takes to be different kinds, or "types," of things, events, people, etc. The *reliability* of what you are thinking is a *probability* between zero and 100 percent that you are right about each of these defining traits. For example, that the person who stole your backpack was not only male, blond, but also unusually tall. If you are wrong about any one of them, then the reliability of what you are thinking is directly affected. (b) WHY? or RELATIONAL thinking is your brain's way of trying to make sense of what it is experiencing, or might experience, by asking what could be the reasons, or causes (labeled here as natural, invented, and necessary), explaining such observations or results. While all of the possible reasons considered might be responsible, as the reliability guide shows, they may not all contribute equally to the observed or anticipated outcomes. © John Edward Terrell.   27

1.3. "Trial of a sow and pigs at Lavegny" in 1457. Robert Chambers (1869) *The Book of Days: A Miscellany of Popular Antiquities in Connection with the Calendar, Including Anecdote, Biography, & History, Curiosities of Literature and Oddities of Human Life and Character,* page 128: "Our artist has endeavoured to represent this scene; but we fear that his sense of the ludicrous has incapacitated him for giving it with the due solemnity." Public domain, via Wikimedia Commons.   29

1.4. An example of a visual IQ test question used to measure what is said to be general human intelligence and abstract reasoning, User:Life of Riley, CC BY-SA 3.0, via Wikimedia Commons. 37

1.5. An alchemist in his laboratory. Conrad Gessner (1599), *The practise of the new and old phisicke, wherein is contained the most excellent secrets of phisicke and philosophie, deuided into foure bookes*, London, Peter Short. Before the discovery of the chemical element oxygen at the end of the eighteenth century, it was widely believed that there was a fire-like element called *phlogiston* inside combustible materials that was released when they burned. (As an aside, Gessner is generally also credited with the invention of the pencil.) Public Domain Mark, via Wellcome Collection. 38

2.1. Understanding how and why things are the way they are at any given time calls for weighing the roles not only of chance and necessity but also choice. © John Edward Terrell. 43

2.2. How variable or predictable we end up being [3] in how we behave differs according to the four famous scholars we have discussed in this chapter. (a) For B. F. Skinner and other behavioral psychologists, the likelihood that what we do will be repeated depends on whether what we have done has been positively or negatively reinforced (rewarded), and not on whether we chose to do what happened. (b) Clifford Geertz, on the other hand, grants us the freedom to decide what to do, but even so, we must be taught by others how to behave properly and well. (c) In contrast, Herbert Simon grants that we can make choices in life, but he assumes the choices we make are ones reflecting the demands and opportunities of the world around us. (d) Like Simon, Daniel Kahneman insists that how intelligent we are reveals how rational we are—how closely attuned we are to things and events outside the limits of our skulls. But more so than Simon, he cautions that good answers to life's questions may take more work than we may want to invest in being successful. © John Edward Terrell. 56

3.1. (a) Phrenological chart, *Webster's Academic Dictionary*, circa 1895. Public domain, via Wikimedia Commons. (b) Different brain structures involved in the recognition of a word and an emotional expression observed using functional MRI. Gray-tone adaptation, Shima Ovaysikia, Khalid A. Tahir, Jason L. Chan and Joseph F.X. DeSouza, CC BY 2.5, via Wikimedia Commons. 63

3.2. Three basic abilities of the human brain when you are dealing with the world around you (and also with your own aches and pains). (1) Attending to what is going on is a balance between awareness, recognition, and imagination in which attending to things and events outside your skull dominates. (2) Converting your bodily sensations into useful information by connecting them with what you already know through your previous experiences. (3) Trying to make sense of what is evidently happening or could happen. These three mental functions are sometimes conscious, but not necessarily so. Moreover, in different situations, we rely on these three neurological talents in different ways. For example, when we are daydreaming, we dial down how aware we are of what is happening around us. Some might say these three are different and distinct "cognitive modules" (Bolhuis et al. 2011), but in reality no one knows how these functions are performed by the brain. It is more than likely that they can be done more or less simultaneously, although not necessarily all with an equal commitment of your brain's resources. For further discussion, see: Terrell and Terrell 2020. © John Edward Terrell. 65

3.3. A gray-tone version of an Ishihara color test panel (numeral 2 in pale green on pink dotted background). The Ishihara color test for detecting red-green vision deficiencies is named after its inventor Dr. Shinobu Ishihara at the University of Tokyo, who first published his tests in 1917. It is a well-recognized fact that the real world does not have the colors our eyes tell us are "out there" to be seen, and not all of us "see" the same colors. Sakurambo, CC BY-SA 3.0, via Wikimedia Commons. 68

3.4. What are memories made of? (a) True-to-life raster image of a wolf (this is a 2.36 MB, 300 dpi, jpg image; Source: Steve, Pexel, Public Domain); (b) simplified version of this same image that is unclear about what sort of an animal is being seen—ambiguity that could lead to making a fatal decision (1.89 MB, 300 dpi, jpg image); (c) minimal trace of the same image conveying a critical impression of what you are dealing with in a simplified way (322 KB, 300 dpi, jpg image). © John Edward Terrell. 77

3.5. Although some psychologists during the twentieth century were willing to analyze the behavior of animals, including human beings, as the pairing of a stimulus with a particular response, even then it was widely recognized that individuals play critical roles in what happens to them (Woodworth and Schlosberg 1954). Adopting our terminology, functional awareness can be thought of as going down five steps, or stages, of engagement with the world beyond the confines of the skull. © John Edward Terrell. 90

4.1. In this book, we suggest that acting intelligently can be thought of as a dynamic interplay of mental skills on three different levels of engagement with the opportunities we have and challenges we face in life. © John Edward Terrell. 98

4.2. MOTIS test. Reprinted with permission, New Zealand Educational Institute. 103

4.3. A *jugaad* vehicle from Gujarat called *chakda*. © Abhik Ghosh. 105

Tables

0.1. Intelligence redefined as three levels of awareness. © John Edward Terrell. 20

2.1. All four of these famous scholars have interpreted intelligence to mean how effectively someone is able to achieve their goals. Both Simon and Kahneman, who were awarded the Sveriges Riksbank Prize in Economic Sciences in Memory of Alfred Nobel for their work, have described our success at making our own choices in life as one of the hallmarks of our evolutionary success as a species. © John Edward Terrell. 45

3.1. Everyday examples of situational and sequential memory traces. © John Edward Terrell. 77

3.2. Defining ingredients of intelligence as seen from differing perspectives on what it means to be human. © John Edward Terrell. 87

3.3. Intelligence reinterpreted as levels of awareness. © John Edward Terrell. 88

4.1. Three basic questions. 111

Acknowledgments

While we were writing this book, we often asked for comments from John Terrell's Facebook friends about what we were trying to put into writing. We want to thank them for helping us in this way.

Rebecca Ackermann, Khaled Ali, Levin Ahmed, Jennifer Alexander, Jalal Al-hajji, Tricia Allen, Andrea Alveshere, John Angel, Josephine Makeso Baig, Aditya Banerjee, Dhritiman Bardalai, Dilwara Begum, Samir Behara, Bob Benfer, Brad Biglow, Benjamin Blount, Susan Blum, Sandra Bowdler, Mark Staff Brandl, Dan Brinkmeier, J. P. Brown, Joyce Chelberg, Jeffrey Clark, Jane Connolly, Helen Dawson Craig Deller, Macaxko Demyan, Deepak Dhankhar, Ashwani Dixit, Reynald Leeu Dixon, Miranilda Duarte, Fadwa El Guindi, Catherine Ellyin, Sweta Federer, Robin Ferruggia, Kathy Fine, Kerim Friedman, Robert Gania, Thomas Gara, Mimi George, Tom Gerald, Duryyodhan Ghosh, Almira Astudillo Gilles, Kate Gillogly, Marisa Giorgi, James Goff, Anna Goldman, Lynne Goldstein, Coniah Gorona, Julie Gough, Chris Green, Bion Griffin, Sebastian Haraha, Harriet Hart, David Herdrich, Jane Hickman, Shashikanta Hidangmayum, Eddie Hill, Sue Hodges, Sun-Kee Hong, John Hoopes, Michael Horvich, MD Sipon Hossain, Jennifer Huff, Damien Huffer, Helga Ingeborg Vierich, Nishant Jindal, Vikki John, A. P. Johnson, Dharamveer Kapoor, Janet Dixon Keller, Carol Kellogg, Cheryl Mills Kelly, Mark Kennedy, Ronald Kephart, Muhammad Shehzad Khan, Priti Khan, Mark Kissel, Susanne Kuehling, Tridip Kuila, Ann McInnis Oates Laffey, Steve Langlois, Becky Lao, Dashka LB, San-San Liu, Jacob Wainwright Love, Katie MacKinnon-Burks, Mark Madsen, Ralph Reeves Angiwa Mana, Jon Marks, Wemin Harau Maropo, Neal Matherne, Arvin Raj Mathur, John McCarthy, Lois McCarthy-Robinson, Ruben Mendoza, Susan Meswick, Richard Milner, Danfordio Mohammed, Theresy Moses, Julie Mota, Anjan Mukherjee, Sanjoy Mukherjee, Michelle Murin, Joel

Tony Mwala, Neha Neha, Margaret Nelson, Markku Niskanen, Oskar Nowak, Robin Öberg, Millie Beth Ojeda, Nick Orange, Arunesh Pandey, Elly Maria Papamichael, Jim Patternson, Mike Pavlik, Sarah Pollock, Jill Pruetz, Amy Pulo, Toshihiro Barreto Ramirez, Joshua Ray's, Scotty Retu, Bill Rosoman, Anamika Roy, Asit Roy, Biplab Roy, Esther Schechter, Tory Schendel-Vyvoda, Robert Shaw, Peter Sheppard, Susan Guise Sheridan, Mukesh Singh, Neetu Singh, Victor Vida Sonoling, Todd Ian Stark, J. A. Sterling, Estevez Stvz, Kasia Szremski, At Tainur Islam Tain, Laura Tamakoshi, Joe Tara, Margaret Thayer, Gayle Timmerman, शुभम् कुमार तिवारी, Dirk Van Tuerenhout, Roger VonStrophenheimer, Lisa Wagner, Khaled Ben Walid, Christopher Wambede, David Whitlock, Chandana Withanachchi, John Wolf, Eleanor Wynn, Alex Xela, Karminn Daytec Yañgot, Dilyana Ivanova Zieske, Amy Zillman.

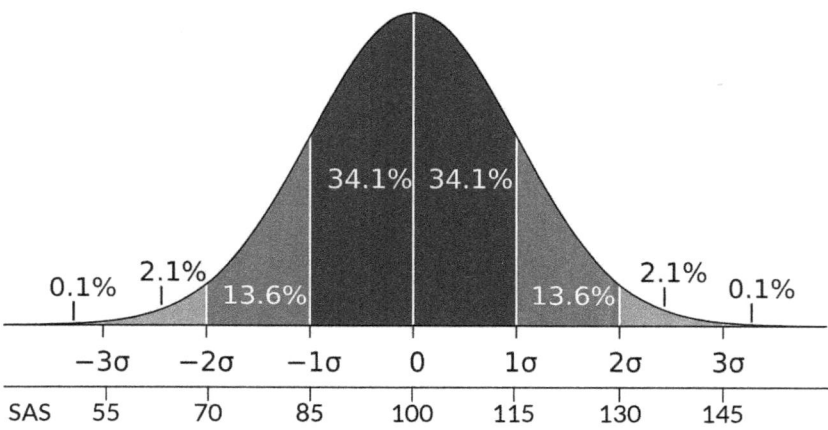

Figure 0.1. Normalized distribution of IQ on the Wechsler Adult Intelligence Scale (WAIS) with a mean of 100 and a standard deviation 15. It is commonly assumed by many today that, like a person's height and weight, their intelligence can be measured to discover how smart they are stacked up against other people. When charted as a normal distribution, approximately 68 percent of adults are believed to fall within one standard distribution above and below the mean. Dmcq, CC BY-SA 3.0, via Wikimedia Commons.

Introduction

WHAT IS INTELLIGENCE?

There is little agreement today on what the word *intelligence* means. Yet this word is widely believed to be about something real, mostly biological, and important. Looked at closely, however, it turns out this word belongs more in the realm of traditional folklore than modern science.

Nobody can say for sure what intelligence means. What this word implies seems clear enough when used in the arena of military or industrial intelligence: it means collecting and analyzing information. But how the basic question "What is this?" otherwise gets answered often makes it sound as if intelligence is far more than simply having a sizable number of facts and figures. Judging by popular wisdom and protracted debates on social media, this familiar word evidently refers to nothing less than our inherited biological ability as human beings to be not only wise but wonderfully successful at whatever we set our sights on doing.

Moreover, intelligence is evidently something—whatever it is—that can be scientifically measured, weighed, and even cut up, or subdivided, into different types or categories of more specialized things, whatever they are, much like the different types of muscles in your body (Bornstein 2020: 125, 126; Davis et al. 2011; Gottfredson 1997). From this popular perspective, intelligence is also something you can have a lot of, and luckily find yourself being labeled a genius (Simonton 2021); or sadly, something you do not have nearly enough of, and so find yourself being seen by others, at least behind your back, as silly, stupid, or plainly idiotic.

Even in the latter case, however, it is commonly said that by merely being human, we are all unquestionably the most intelligent, the most wise, the most rational of all the world's life forms, past and present. Is this true? Is there something about human intelligence that makes all of us the most remarkable, the most intelligent creatures on Earth—and possibly even in the Universe?

When answering questions of this sort, it is often taken for granted that the right answers are likely to be straightforward and categorical. Yes, intelligence is something that can be measured, weighed, and subdivided. Yes, we are the most rational creatures on Earth. Yes, there is something unusual, something special about human intelligence making all of us as a species remarkably brainy and insightful—fully equipped, in other words, to rule the world and be the masters of our own fate. No wonder, therefore, the Swedish naturalist Carl Linnaeus in 1758 gave us our modern scientific name *Homo sapiens*, Latin for "wise man" (Agamben 2001: 23)

Are we really this special? Or is this wishful thinking on our part? If they could speak, would chimpanzees and bonobos, our closest biological relatives, agree with us?

Reasons for Doubt

All of the authors of this book are anthropologists and historians. We all have done research in different parts of the world. We all have an abiding interest in documenting what it means to be human. We decided to write this book together because we know firsthand what people will tell you it takes to be smart and capable as a human being cannot be boiled down to the singular (or even multiple) "something" that many in Europe and North America—academically trained, or not—will claim can legitimately be labeled (sometimes scornfully) as "intelligence." Yet more bewildering, even people in Europe and North America do not agree on what this word in the English language means.

The *Cambridge Dictionary* defines *intelligence* as "the ability to learn, understand, and make judgments or have opinions that are based on reason." This same dictionary defines *reason* as knowing "the cause of an event or situation or something that provides an excuse or explanation." How useful these seemingly uncomplicated definitions are will be considered more fully in Chapter 1. In the same chapter, we survey how human intelligence has been seen throughout much of the Global North down through history and in philosophy, psychology, and the popular press.

Defining intelligence as the ability to learn, understand, and explain events and situations does not necessarily imply that we are able to do so skillfully and well. After all, it may be easy enough to judge how successfully someone is able to get something done (say, quickly adding numbers), but how do you judge what they think about something?

Therefore, also discussed in Chapter 1 is the popular claim that how smart you are can be measured (and judged) by how well you can find patterns hidden in numbers, picture puzzles, word lists, and the like. Ex-

> ### Is It Really Saltimbocca?
>
>
>
> Metaphorically speaking, intelligence is like the Italian dish "saltimbocca." If you google the term or consult a cookbook, you will find a variety of definitions, and if you order the dish in Italian restaurants around the world, it turns out, amazingly, that there is not one single common ingredient in the dishes served as "saltimbocca." Still, there are experts who claim they know and other experts who admit they do not know for certain, but they believe nevertheless there must be a definition (and they may still be working on one).
>
> De Boeck, Gore, Gonzalez, and Martin. 2020. "An Alternative View on the Measurement of Intelligence and Its History."
>
> Saltimbocca alla Romana. Alec Vuijlsteke, CC BY 2.0, via Wikimedia Commons

perts in psychology, behavioral economics, and other academic fields often caution, however, that all of us use mental shortcuts when faced with everyday problems we somehow need to solve, perhaps quickly, perhaps not. There is even a technical word for these hasty and potentially flawed strategies that cannot be guaranteed to give us true and correct solutions for dealing with the realities of life. They are labeled as *heuristic strategies*, or just *heuristics* (Gigerenzer 2020; Gigerenzer and Gaissmaier 2011; Kahneman 2011; Weinberger and Stoycheva 2020).

All human thought, however, is basically impressionistic and prone to error. Therefore, the real issue is what can be done to keep the magnitude of human error reasonably in check.

How Intelligent Is This?

Instead of simply taking it for granted that intelligence can be defined as the ability to learn, understand, and make judgments or have opinions based on reason, it is important to acknowledge that there is considerable evidence, both historical and in today's news, attesting to the seemingly countless ways we all can stumble intellectually and end up not being nearly as clever as we may want to believe we are. There are many good reasons to doubt how smart we are as a species, however promising the label Linnaeus gave us. Here are five examples.

1. Astronomy

John Terrell's high school Physics teacher favored saying that "the obvious is seldom seen." Another way of saying much the same thing is to say "it's easy to take things for granted." Furthermore, familiarity may not necessarily breed contempt, but it can lead us to overlook the wisdom in the old saying that appearances can be deceiving. Rather than spurring us to take a closer look, we may not even see the value of doing so.

Consider, for example, a famous case from the history of astronomy. Recognition that we are not living strategically located at the center of the Universe is often credited to Nicholas Copernicus in the sixteenth century. In fact, however, as the astronomer Owen Gingerich wrote years ago, there were even those in ancient Greece who had already gone against appearances in favor of the seemingly counterfactual truth of a sun-centered (heliocentric) model of our solar system (Gingerich 1973). Furthermore, he made it clear that Copernicus had known their arguments, and had said so in his famous book *De revolutionibus orbium coelestium* (*On the Revolutions of the Heavenly Spheres*), first published shortly before his death in 1543.

It is often also added that the model of our solar system proposed by Copernicus as an alternative to conventional wisdom was far from accurate or convincing (Gingerich 2004). It was the seventeenth century astronomer Johannes Kepler who finally suspected that the orbits of the planets are not circular but instead elliptical. This realization led him to propose his now famous three laws of planetary motion. Yet, it was still not until Isaac Newton advanced his theory of universal gravitation in *Principia Mathematica* (1687) that the heliocentric view began to win out over the seemingly obvious older earth-centered (geocentric) model of the universe (Figure 0.3).

2. Salem Witch Trials

Despite the popular claim that we are superior to all other creatures on Earth, we have an obvious intellectual handicap. Try as we might, we cannot read minds. The only way we are able to tell what others are thinking and why—and not just others who are human, but others such as family pets, lions, tigers, and bears—is to watch and listen to what they do, say, or in some way vocalize (Terrell and Terrell 2020). Because of this genuine disability, it can be hard, if not always impossible, to figure out why others do, or did, what they are doing, or have done.

The case of the famous Salem witch trials of 1692–1693 is no exception. What happened then in and around Salem, Massachusetts, seems well documented historically, at least the basic details. Between February 29 1692 and May 1693, an astonishing number of people were accused

Figure 0.2. Claudius Ptolemy, a Greek mathematician, astronomer, and geographer who lived in Alexandria in the 2nd century A.D. His mathematical arguments were so influential that the ancient Earth-centered view of the universe is known today as the Ptolemaic system. Picture from a sixteenth century book frontispiece. Theodor de Bry, Public domain, via Wikimedia Commons.

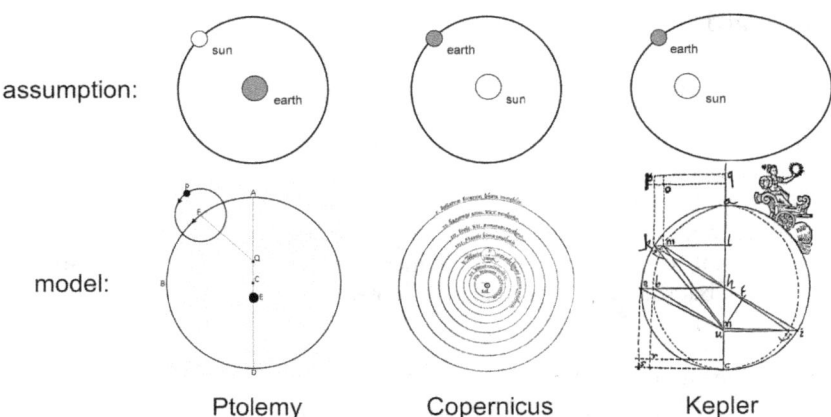

Figure 0.3. The decisive role of prior assumptions. What we take for granted can play a decisive role, for example, in how we see our place in the Universe. Bottom row, left: Muhammad, CC BY-SA 3.0, via Wikimedia Commons; middle: Public domain, Wikimedia Commons; right: Arthur Berry (1862-1929), Public domain, Wikimedia Commons. © John Edward Terrell

of witchcraft, and twenty were executed. The uproar began when two girls, one nine years old and the other eleven, started having "fits." A local doctor asserted that an evil hand was at work, not natural causes. Then, another young girl began to act similarly. When questioned by local magistrates, these girls blamed three women: a homeless beggar, a Caribbean slave, and an elderly and impoverished woman. Two of the women insisted they were innocent. The Caribbean woman, however, apparently confessed to having been recruited by the Devil. All three women were sent to jail.

Thereafter, others were also accused of evil deeds, mostly by a core group of girls and young women, although others, too, stepped forward to relate strange and mysterious events, some going back decades. On June 10, the first of those accused was found guilty and hanged as a witch on what was later known as Gallows Hill. Five more people were hanged in July, five in August, and eight in September. By the middle of May the following year when the crisis ended, nineteen people having been accused of signing the Devil's Book—thereby becoming "a detestable Witch"—had been hanged, one old man had been crushed to death with heavy stones, others had died in jail, and over two-hundred people had been accused of practicing the Devil's magic.

Ironically, although in previous witchcraft trials back in Europe confessing to doing the Devil's evil work had usually led to execution, this time around confession became a way to escape the gallows. Needless to say, this led to many confessions. Those, however, who defiantly proclaimed their innocence were more than likely found guilty, and some were hanged.

What was the nature of the incriminating evidence against so many? In the words of one recent commentator:

> Two particularly strong themes emerge from the trial documents and the observer and commentator accounts: spectral evidence and confessions. Much of the evidence presented, especially by the core group, relied on spectral affliction: the afflicted claimed to be tormented by the accused in spectral form. Naturally, this evidence could not be independently verified, but the court nevertheless accepted its legitimacy. (Grund 2020: 74)

What are we to make of what took place long ago at Salem in the Province of Massachusetts Bay (which was to become one of the first thirteen states in the United States of America)? Several probable explanations have been advanced over the years as to why what happened then occurred. These include everything from family feuds and local politics to mass hysteria. Regardless of the cause or causes and personal motives of those involved, what stands out is that accusations of witchcraft and being in league with the Devil were taken seriously enough that dire consequences could most decidedly result.

The biologist and Nobel Laureate François Jacob titled his popular book on science and evolution *The Possible and The Actual* (1982). If you read this short and insightful book, you soon learn that the word "possible" in its title refers to how the human mind tries to decide what can or cannot be true in the real world. From this perspective, what remains unclear is whether people in Salem in 1692 genuinely believed in the potency of witchcraft and the Devil's magic to threaten the public order, or alternatively, were simply willing to invoke the alleged efficacy of both to advance their own private and political ends. Yet even if we could still ask them, how would we know for sure they were telling us the truth?

3. Conspiracy Theories

Not being able to read minds is not the only obvious intellectual handicap we all have as human beings. Try as we might, we also cannot be an eyewitness to all events and decisions affecting our lives and shaping our success as clever creatures.

Political events in recent years in the United States have made the phrase "conspiracy theory" a part of everyday life for many of us. The evident willingness on the part of some to believe rumors and accept hearsay evidence undoubtedly contributed to the mob attack on the United States Capitol Building in Washington, D.C., on January 6, 2021, although exactly why this shocking event happened will probably be one of history's enduring questions.

There is no need here to detail or resolve this recent chapter in the conduct of political life in the United States. The point to be made instead is this one: we may be smart in many ways, but telling the difference between what is real and what is only plausible is harder for all of us to do as observant and skillful beings than conventional wisdom and common sense may lead us to believe. To repeat: we cannot read minds, and we cannot witness firsthand all that we might need to know to always be able to tell fact from fiction, truth from falsehood, honest claims and downright lies.

4. How Not to Catch a Cold

Possibly the most widespread medical belief on earth is the idea that cold winds can make you sick. The common expression "catch a cold" immortalizes this idea, which is still believed by millions of people. Even those who know about rhinoviruses and the like often argue that the viruses are always around, and a cold wind can definitely make them attack—especially if you go outside with wet hair, or without your coat.

The origins of this popular idea may lie in the basic fact that hypothermia (when your body loses heat faster than you produce it) and hyperthermia (when your body becomes dangerously overheated) can definitely be deadly without needing the assistance of a virus. However, the most that can be said is that although being cold and wet do not cause colds, both colder temperatures and drier air may independently or jointly contribute to the risk of human rhinovirus (HRV) infections, either by altering the survival and spread of viruses in the environment, or by affecting our susceptibility to infection (Ikäheimo et al. 2016).

A related Chinese belief holds that too much internal heat causes dryness and sores in the mouth and throat, plus weakness, skin problems, and susceptibility to disease. The cure is to eat cooling foods—green vegetables and herbs. These symptoms are classically those of the disease called scurvy (below, Conclusion), for which the cure of vitamin-rich foods is perfect. Although the ancient Chinese would not have known about Vitamin C, they saw that this change in diet was beneficial. This was not so, however, when they tried to treat scurvy with dried herbs, or use green vegetables to treat infectious diseases having scurvy-like symptoms (Anderson 1980, 1984, 2007, 2014).

5. *Racism, Foreign Colonialism, and African Science*

Many Europeans have long seen skin color as a sign of intelligence. The lighter you are in your appearance, the smarter, more progressive, and technologically more advanced you are, and vice versa. As the bioanthropologist Nina Jablonski has remarked: "Skin color was the keystone trait to which other physical, behavioral, and culture characteristics were linked" (Jablonski 2021: 437): While there have been many examples, Immanuel Kant's notorious remark about a black carpenter sums up such thinking even if Kant himself may not have wanted to be taken seriously: "but in short, this fellow was quite black from head to foot, a clear proof that what he said was stupid" (White 2013: 542).

By late medieval times in Europe, blackness was associated with evil or something inherently defective, undesirable, or mysterious while whiteness was taken as a sign of goodness, desirability, and honesty. Being dark-skinned easily invoked distrust and suspicions of cannibalism, devilishness, and inferiority. Like the phoenix bird, these attitudes have an enduring shelf-life even in our own times. The psychiatrist, political philosopher, and Marxist Frantz Fanon aptly captured in his writings the prejudiced thinking and practice that empties the black body of all forms of humanity and sees blackness as a curse that blacks should desire to escape from (Fanon 2008).

Nowadays, such attitudes are still called racist, but it is not clear which gave birth to the other: racism or the fallacious equation linking black skin color with stupidity. Fanon has used an anecdote about when a white child pointed at him and declared "Look, a Negro!" to examine what lies behind this loaded racial slur. Borrowing Jean-Paul Sartre's "white gaze argument" (Stoneman 2023), he says racism brands black people in a way white people do not face, and stereotypes blacks as bad, mean, and ugly animals or cannibals (Fanon 2008).

In 2007, James D. Watson, the Chicago-born, 1953 DNA structure co-discoverer, and 1962 Nobel Prize for Medicine winner, told a British journalist that the prospect of Africa was inherently gloomy because "all our social policies are based on the fact that their intelligence is the same as ours—whereas all the testing says not really." Though he hoped that everyone is equal, "people who have to deal with black employees find this is not true." When asked how long it might take for the genes leading to differences in human intelligence to be identified, his answer: "15 years. However, he wonders if even 10 years will pass" (Hunt-Grubbe 2007).

Like Watson's notorious remarks, debate about black vs. white intelligence often focuses on biology and genetics, not on science and technology. When it comes to the latter, however, both words can have many meanings and interpretations. Seeing both only from a European point of view ignores the reality that people around the world may not only do things differently, but also have other purposes and goals in mind.

In Western nations, science is often performed in well-documented and controlled environments that are called *laboratories*. Historically, this has not always been the case, and the European "scientific method" is a relatively recent phenomenon (Mavhunga 2017). Furthermore, the documentation created as part of the "scientific method" ensures the reproducibility of results in accord with the "laws of science" as understood in Western epistemology.

It is not surprising, therefore, that when European travelers increasingly found themselves encountering Africans after 1492, they expected to find people doing things not only the way they were being done in Europe, but also making things the way they were making them there. Instead, although not widely known today, they found people in Africa were using what came across to these foreign travelers and traders as decidedly unfamiliar and strangely ritualized methods of transforming iron ore into useful metal. People there were also following recipes that apparently had not been written out to be passed down from one generation to the next.

In Western eyes, there seemed to be only two ways to explain such seemingly odd behavior. Africans were either not really doing science at all, but rather something akin to magic or voodoo. Or what they were doing so strangely was a degenerated version of what they had learned from an ancient and superior race that had long ago vanished from the face of the Earth (Bandama 2013). Either way, Europeans were associating African practices with skin color and seeing Africans as lesser beings than themselves.

The ironic fact is that as we now learn more and more about the history of science and technology, it is becoming clearer that Africa has been home, for instance, to remarkable technological diversity in metallurgical skills both in terms of methods and finished products. The unique downdraught iron furnace technology of the Mandara people of Cameroon (David et al. 1989) is an easily overlooked example. Like other bloomery technology (traditional smelting involving the melting of impurities leaving a sponge iron bloom), this is a solid-state reduction technology, but it uses an exceptionally long blowpipe (*tuyere*) inserted vertically deep into the furnace to serve the dual purpose of facilitating both slag formation as the ore melts and feeding oxygen to the furnace for combustion (Killick 2015).

The African diversity in metallurgical processes and products speaks to the little-known fact that Africans knew how to produce metals thousands of years before European colonialism. In fact, some parts of West and Central Africa had probably developed the world's first iron technology (Chirikure 2015). This happened without the apprenticeship stage which characterized the gradual Eurasian transition from simpler copper metallurgy to complex iron technology. Even during the later years of contact, many Eurasian explorers considered African metals to be much better in quality than metals in their places of origin.

The history of metallurgy in Africa and the innovations made there all involved stages now associated also with modern science (observation, question, experimentation, analysis, conclusions, and repeatability). Unlike in Europe, however, where keeping written records was standard and usual, in Africa, how to turn ore into useful metal was knowledge shared and passed down from one generation to another in non-written ways such as songs, practical observations, and accompanying rituals. And yet Western colonial officials derided African non-written achievements as backward and barbaric. Although this was done under the guise of civilizing "barbaric Africa," here is another example of how factual ignorance can trump historical truth. And thereby lead to feelings of racial superiority on the part of some that are actually the product of ignorance.

Figure 0.4. The down-draught iron smelting furnace near Kasungu, Malawi. The stack is made of baked clay taken from termite mounds and is sufficiently high to permit the furnace to attain smelting temperature by natural draft rather than with an air blast provided by pumping bellows. Source: David J. Killick, used with permission.

Rethinking Intelligence

These five examples, drawn both from history and what is happening today, support what social scientists and others have long been saying. People around the world often use remarkably different ways to explain things, events, and why people do what they do (Alcoff 2007; Mignolo 2007). Moreover, the notion that some people are inherently far superior to the usual run of the rest of us at learning, understanding, and making judgments or having opinions based on reason may sound right, but this definition of intelligence ignores an old and famously difficult question, as well as plentiful evidence to the contrary.

QUESTION: What is Truth?

According to one religious website on the internet: "truth is simply telling it like it is; it is the way things really are, and any other viewpoint is wrong. A foundational principle of philosophy is being able to discern between truth and error, or as Thomas Aquinas observed, 'it is the task of the philosopher to make distinctions'" ("What is truth" 2023).

Even if most philosophers as a rule might be willing to say yes, they are seeking after the Truth, this claim about their calling is questionable. Philosophers are famous, after all, for arguing, often vehemently, about whether they or anyone else has ever found it. Therefore, claiming somebody is more intelligent than other people because they are better equipped biologically to know the truth when they come across it (e.g., H. J. Eysenck *in* Sternberg 1984: 290–91) sounds more like wishful thinking than a credible way to certify somebody as a genius.

EVIDENCE

Both individually and when we get together with others of our kind, we are all perfectly capable of believing, often quite strongly so, the most incredible things. Current research on what is perhaps all too easily called "artificial intelligence" (AI) generally takes it for granted that intelligence is about being able to successfully find the right answers to mathematical, verbal, and spatial puzzles (Biever 2023). But what does it mean to fail such tests of intelligence? What are the consequences? Why is Truth not only famous for being elusive, but also easy to overlook or take for granted? Why is it apparently so easy to ignore what would seem obvious, and instead believe with passionate conviction delusions, deliberate fictions, and downright lies?

Therefore, if intelligence is a measure of how successfully we can find "the cause of an event or situation or something that provides an excuse or explanation," then the latter half of this definition of the word reason makes sense—although equally good words to use would be rationalize and rationalization. Yet, as shown by the five examples just given, the notion that some of us are smart enough to see the truth that the rest of us are too stupid to grasp does not square with the history and current condition of our species. If this were not so, there would be no need to write this book.

In the following chapters, therefore, we survey briefly some of what has been said about human intelligence from historical, philosophical, psychological, and political points of view (Chapter 1). Then, four different ways of thinking about what it means to behave intelligently are summarized and compared (Chapter 2). Following this closer look at these popular theories, we describe (Chapter 3) a way to understand how all of us think about things and our own hopes and wants taking into account how inventive and creative—both intentionally. and sometimes quite unknowingly—all of us can be as we make our way through life. In the final chapter (Conclusion), we summarize what has been discussed, and offer several suggestions about how to make the most of the real talents all of us possess as bona fide human beings.

To not keep you in the dark, however, here are six of our observations about what has been called intelligence that we will be exploring with you in the following chapters.

Our Conclusions

The common thread running through many definitions of what the word intelligence means is the assumption that however this word is defined, it refers to something which is mostly biological that determines how *effectively* we are able to deal with the world around us (Nickerson 2020: 225). There are good reasons to challenge this conventional idea. It is more useful to think of intelligence as how *aware* we are of what is happening—and may happen down the road—outside the confines of our skulls.

1. Your Brain Is Not a Camera

It is estimated that the human brain contains ~86 billion neurons. This may sound like a lot, but given all that a brain does to keep us alive and well, and given the metabolic cost of using your brain, it is hardly surprising our memories—whatever these are taken to be as physical traces of our experiences as we live and breathe—are generally only as detailed as they need to be to see us through life from day to day (Girard, Jiang, and van Rossum 2023; Kristjánsson and Egeth 2019; Seger and Millar 2010). Moreover, it is not clear how often our memories, however impressionistic or richly inscribed they may be, are (or need to be) updated. There is more than a little truth, therefore, in the saying "if it looks like a duck, swims like a duck, and quacks like a duck, then it probably is a duck," even if what you are dealing with isn't a duck at all. These observations have profound implications for how accurate and trustworthy our understandings of the world are likely to be.

2. Your Brain is Not a Computer

The popularity nowadays of computers, cell phones, and the like encourages us to believe the brain is a kind of organically constructed computer (Cobb 2020; Cosmides and Tooby 1997). As Robert Epstein has observed: "Our shoddy thinking about the brain has deep historical roots, but the invention of computers in the 1940s got us especially confused. For more than half a century now, psychologists, linguists, neuroscientists and other experts on human behavior have been asserting that the human brain works like a computer." His frustration with those who think this way about thinking is obvious. Yes, human babies are born with certain ready-made reactions to particular sorts of stimuli that are important for their survival.

> But here is what we are *not* born with: *information, data, rules, software, knowledge, lexicons, representations, algorithms, programs, models, memories, images, processors, subroutines, encoders, decoders, symbols,* or *buffers*—design elements that allow digital computers to behave somewhat intelligently. Not only are we not *born* with such things, we also don't *develop* them—ever. (Epstein 2016)

Needless to say, not everyone agrees with him (as many of the online comments added to his essay demonstrate). The point we want to make here, however, is that despite the popularity of saying our brains are like computers, it is fundamentally misleading to say, as so many nowadays do (Friston 2008, 2016; Friston et al. 2017), that our brains are constantly trying to *predict* what will happen next, and we are constantly *computing the probability* of this or that happening. Far better words to use are *expect* and having *expectations* derived simply from your prior experiences.

The saying "experience is the best teacher" has been around at least since the time of Julius Caesar and other famous Romans of long ago. We are confident someone suffering from PTSD (Post-traumatic stress disorder) might strongly disagree. Even so, our point is this one. The experiences we have in life lead us to have useful expectations about what may happen next. These foreshadowings of what may happen are not statistical, and they do not literally require us to do computations of any sort. Instead, we are skilled at finding *patterns* in the things and events "out there" in what many would call the "real world."

3. Intelligence is Not About Success

What we know about the world around us is mostly just "good enough" for us to get by from day to day. No wonder, therefore, that it can be hard work to memorize something as complex as Beethoven's *Moonlight Sonata in C-sharp minor*. No wonder, too, witnesses during jury trials may not necessarily get their facts right, and may instead testify to something they believe happened because in hindsight this is what they honestly think must have happened.

Robert Sternberg, who has written often about how important it is to capitalize on our strengths and compensate for, or correct, our weaknesses, has argued repeatedly that even if there is no agreement on what the word means, "intelligence involves formulating, striving for, and achieving, to the extent possible, a meaningful and coherent set of goals" (Sternberg 2020b: 680; also Sternberg 1999: 438). On the plus side of this way of thinking about intelligence, he is one of many who have pointed out that successful intelligence involves a wider range of human abilities than those assessed by tests of intellectual or academic skills. Yet what is both fascinating and obvious about associating intelligence with success is that being a failure in life does not have to mean you are intellectually stupid. As Keith Stanovich and his colleagues have pointed out, "smart people do foolish things all the time" (Stanovich, Toplak, and West 2020: 1106).

On the other hand, although Stanovich and his colleagues have said that being rational is different from being intelligent, they define rationality in ways that would seem to contradict this claim. "For our beliefs to be rational they must correspond to the way the world is—they must be true (epistemic rationality). For our actions to be rational, they must be the best means toward our goals—they must be the best things to do (instrumental rationality)" (2020: 1109).

Therefore, even if intelligence and rationality are somehow different, we find it hard not to see them as just two sides of the same coin. In this book, we argue instead that the challenge of being human is not how successful or seemingly rational you are, but how willing and able you are to be aware of what is happening around you.

4. Your Brain Is a Pattern Recognition Device

A useful way to think about what it means to say "I think" is to describe what is happening inside your skull begins as *pattern recognition* (Kahneman and Klein 2009; Pi et al. 2008). As Herbert Simon (see Chapter 2) wrote decades ago about the skillfulness of a grandmaster at the game of chess:

> The information associated with familiar patterns may include knowledge about what to do when the pattern is encountered. Thus the experienced chess player who recognizes the feature called an *open file* thinks immediately of the open file possibility of moving a rook to that file. The move may or may not be the best one, but it is one that should be considered whenever an open file is present. The expert recognizes not only the situation in which he finds himself, but also what action might be appropriate for dealing with it. (Simon 1996: 86)

In the above excerpt, Simon wrote about the phenomenon, the kind of thinking, commonly called intuition, and how he felt it could be readily explained: "most intuitive leaps are acts of recognition." Nobody needs to be as skillful at a game called chess to know firsthand that doing something "by intuition" is what all of us often do. The spooky part, of course, is this means you often don't have to realize what you are doing to get it done. This is, of course, a godsend when you are on a bicycle without training wheels.

It is also useful to think about the physical traces of our life experiences filed away in the neurons of that large mass of tissue on top of our shoulders—in this book, we will be referring to these stored experiences as memory traces—in two alternative ways. These traces may be 2- and 3-dimensional spatial mappings of people, places, and the like (we will be calling these traces *situational mappings*). They can also be time traces (*sequential mappings*).

An example of the first kind of memory tracing is learning—and hopefully being able to recall—the right password or pin number that will get you into your computer, cell phone, or online bank account. Another is being able to remember where you left the book you were reading before you started cooking dinner. Examples of the second sort would be what you know might happen if you forget your wedding anniversary, and why you expect a goodnight kiss from your life's partner lying next to you in bed. How well we can remember the details of either sort of neurological mapping will depend on how detailed are the memory traces used, and how altered these traces have become when we have been thinking about them in the past (Cosandi 2016: 54–61).

5. Paying Attention Is Harder than We Think

Not only is the human brain not a camera, it does not work like one. The camera in your cell phone can take richly detailed snapshots of what it is "seeing" in such rapid succession that what it is "capturing" may be turned into videos you can post on social media and replayed whenever you want to do so. In contrast, the retina inside each of your eyeballs has not been designed by evolution (or by God) to accomplish such recording feats. Far from being a biologically constructed photosensitive plate uniformly covered with tiny light sensitive cells, each of which can measure the amount of light falling on it, our retinas are designed to help us pay attention to what is changing in the world around us (Binda and Morrone 2018; Chica et al. 2013). Why? So we can decide—mostly without even having to think about it—whether we need to do something to respond to what we are sensing. The goal, therefore, is not an accurate true-to-life picture or video. Instead, what is sought is a useful one capturing only the details in what we are aware of that our prior experiences have taught us can be ones worth paying attention to, perhaps sometimes even for life-or-death reasons.

David Eagleman, who has written often about neuroscience, has described what the brain is up to when it is attending to the world in this way: "brains reach out and actively *extract* the type of information they

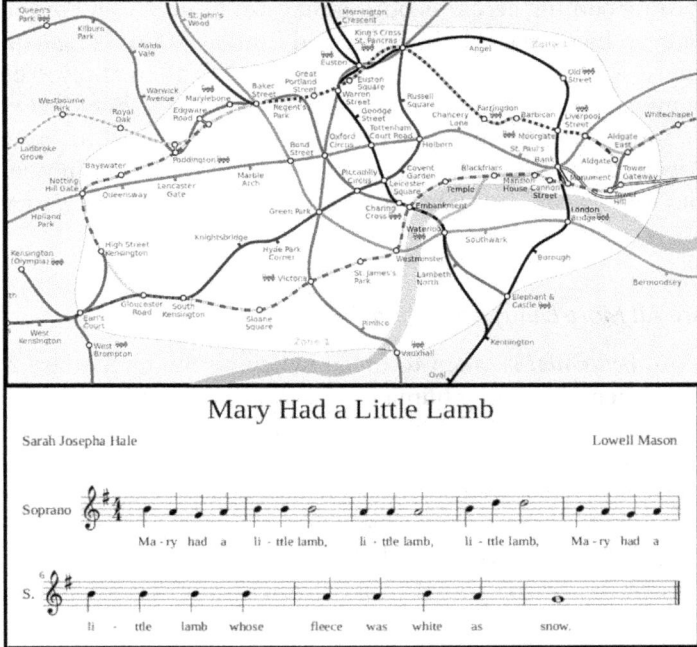

Figure 0.5. (top) Subway map—an example of *situational mapping*. London Underground geographic map, CC 3.0, via Wikimedia Commons. (bottom) Music notation—an example of *sequential mapping*—for "Mary Had a Little Lamb" based on a poem by Sarah Josepha Hale, 1823. Sarah Josepha Hale & Lowell Mason, Public domain, via Wikimedia Commons.

need. The brain does not need to see everything at once . . . it does not need to store everything internally; it only needs to know where to go to find the information." There are surely times when this may be so, but as a general rule, we think this is an overstatement.

After making this claim, Eagleman adds: "As your eyes interrogate the world, they are like agents on a mission, optimizing their strategy for the data" (Eagleman 2011: 30). Moreover, he says, we are all basically unaware that our eyes are thus engaged in such an active, intentional, and secretly deliberate quest for understanding. Again, we think this way of seeing what a brain is normally doing goes too far. Saying, as he does, that vision is active, not passive, overlooks that much of what we take in about the world and then may go on to do is likely to be more habitual than intentional.

Consequently, the downside of having two biologically constructed "environmental sensors" like our eyes located on the sides of your nose is that anything coming across as boring may not be seen as memorable, and may not even be noticed (Liversedge and Findlay 2000). The expressions "been there, done that" and "same old, same old" often apply even if they don't come across as appropriate scientific jargon. What Eagleman has said in a more recent book suggests he has now changed his mind about how actively the brain deliberately needs to weigh whether it needs to go out of its way to find out what is happening around it (Eagleman 2020: 163–73).

6. We Are All More Delusional Than We Believe

If the word *delusional* is taken to mean believing things that are not true, then the challenge of being human is not just seeing things and events for what they are rather than what we believe them to be. It is also easy to be delusional by wrongly assuming what we are experiencing in the here and now is the same as what we have encountered before. There are many familiar expressions for being delusional in this way: "seen one, seen them all," "jumping to conclusions," "been there, done that," and even "can't see the forest for the trees" on the belief you already know what is important and what isn't.

Studying perceptual awareness has long been a major focus in psychology, neuroscience, and nowadays artificial intelligence (AI), too. Despite what common sense tells us, we are never directly in touch with the world around us, but only through our recollections—our memory traces, however recent or longstanding—of what our senses have been picking up, and what our minds have done with these recollections (Seth 2021; Seth and Bayne 2022). As David Eagleman has written, conscious awareness of our surroundings occurs when sensory inputs violate learned expectations. When this hasn't happened, awareness "is not needed because the brain is doing its job well" (Eagleman 2011: 50).

Consequently, deliberately paying attention to what is happening around us can be harder than we think. To paraphrase a well-known saying, if it ain't broke, don't fix it. Like it or not, instead of paying attention to what we are seeing, it is notoriously easy to jump to conclusions that seem to make sense but aren't picking up on what is really "out there" (Figure 0.6).

The reverse—being truly aware of what is happening—can also have its limitations. As we will discuss in Chapter 3, how we deal with the world is a dynamic interplay between *awareness*, *recognition*, and *imagination*. The downside of this constant trialogue, however, can include not "seeing" something happening right before our eyes because we are so preoccupied with attending to something else, lost in our own thoughts, and the like.

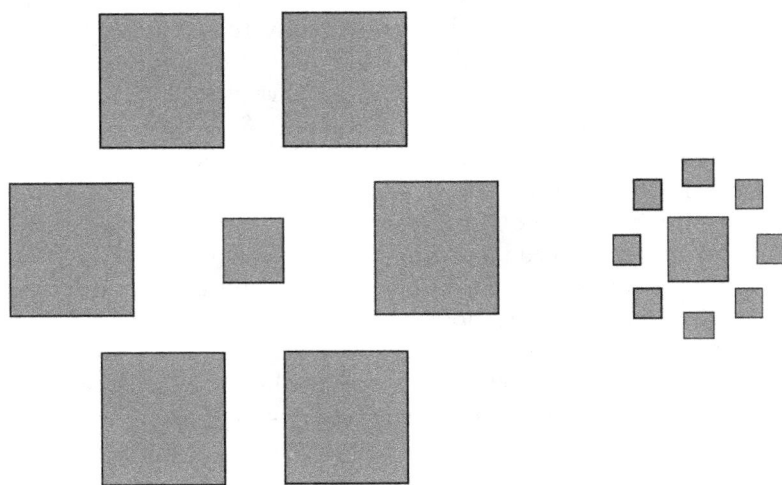

Figure 0.6. Can you tell whether the central square on the right is bigger than the one on the left? Hint: appearances can be deceiving. © John Edward Terrell

Why? Because the human brain can only do so much at any one time. Therefore, what it takes to make us "open our eyes" to what is really going may be something we have only limited control over, and something we should not simply take for granted.

Another way of saying what we have just said is that all of us experience the world filtered through our memories of what we have experienced previously. As we have already said and will discuss again in Chapter 3, our memories of things and events are just our impressions of the world around us of greater or lesser richness. Moreover, to add to our potential woes, our previous impressions—our memory traces—perhaps more likely than not—may have been reworked, perhaps even "corrupted" into reformed memories, fantasies, and hallucinations by what our minds have been doing with them since they were originally formed (Lisman and Sternberg 2013). How delusional they have become may depend on how far they depart from what got them memorized in the first place.

Intelligence Redefined

As human beings, we may see ourselves as remarkably intelligent creatures. All human thought, however, is prone to error. Consequently, what can we do to keep human error reasonably in check? As we have already said, the common thread of many conventional definitions of intelligence is the claim that what is critical is how effectively people deal with the world around them. A more realistic way, however, of pinning down what this word means is the observation that we have three different ways of engaging with what is going on outside the confines of our own skulls: *mechanical awareness, functional awareness,* and *relational awareness.*

In the following chapters, we will spell out why this understanding of what the word intelligence means not only works better than what this word is often taken to mean, but is also a more useful way to think about what makes us who we are. Knowing this can also make it harder for us to be hacked—to use a word popular nowadays when so many of us are taking to the internet and social media to find things out and communicate with one another. Knowing our intellectual weaknesses as well as our strengths can make it harder for others to manipulate us and control our lives.

Table 0.1. Intelligence redefined as 3 levels of awareness. © John Edward Terrell.

INTELLIGENCE LEVEL	A	B	C
mechanical awareness	experience	recognition	imagination
functional awareness	observe	assume	decide
relational awareness	survey	theory	model

Key Points

1. Although there is little agreement today on what it means to be intelligent, this word is widely believed to be about something real, mostly biological, and important.
2. The common thread running through many definitions of what this word means is the assumption that, however defined, it refers to how effectively we can deal with the world around us.
3. There are good reasons to challenge this conventional belief. It is more useful to think of intelligence as how aware we are of what is happening outside the confines of our skulls.

1

Basic Questions

Seeing how often people talk about it, you can be forgiven for thinking what the word *intelligence* means would be something everybody knows and understands. It may come as a shock, therefore, to hear nobody knows for sure what this word is all about and when to use it. Even so, many say intelligence is something you can measure, varies from person to person, and may vary globally, as well, from place to place.

Given how often it is talked about, surely everyone knows and understands what the word intelligence means. On hearing this is not so, we are willing to bet your first reaction was to think we are just being provocative and maybe a little crazy. Before dismissing what we say in this book, consider what one expert on this topic has written. Robert J. Sternberg is widely seen as one of the world's leading authorities on what intelligence is and isn't (Sternberg 2005, 2020b). Yet here is what he said at the end of his chapter on intelligence in the *Cambridge Handbook of Thinking and Reasoning* back in 2005:

> In conclusion, many approaches have been taken to improve understanding of the nature of intelligence. Great progress has been made in elaborating the construct but much less progress in converging upon either a definition or a universally accepted theory. Much of current debate revolves around trying to figure out what the construct is and how it relates to other constructs, such as learning, memory, and reasoning. (Sternberg 2005: 766–67)

You might think this conclusion would be enough to discourage anyone from trying to study intelligence, whatever this is, but Sternberg then immediately went on to add:

Intelligence can be measured, to some extent, and it can be improved. Improvements are not likely to eliminate individual differences, however, because attempts to improve intelligence can help people at all levels and with diverse kinds of intelligence. No matter how high one's intelligence, there is always room for improvement; and no matter how low, there are always measures that can be taken to help raise it.

Fifteen years after these words were published, their author again surveyed what intelligence is and isn't in the *Cambridge Handbook of Intelligence*, a collection of 50 chapters written by 93 different authors for which he served as general editor. Once again he acknowledged that nobody can say for sure what intelligence is. This time around, however, he wrote this is not really an issue, not a problem, mattering all that much.

To explain why he would say this, he began his introduction to this collection of diverse essays by quoting favorably what the poet Gertrude Stein evidently said on her deathbed in 1949: "What is the answer?" On getting no answer, it is reported she then said, "In that case, what is the question?" Sternberg tells us this last question applies to few fields as well as it does to the study of intelligence.

> The source of many of the questions asked about intelligence is the model, or metaphor, that drives research on intelligence. Different metaphors of mind give rise to different questions about the nature of intelligence and about what various empirical phenomena relating to it mean. The field of intelligence has been and continues to be marked by noisy and sometimes vitriolic debates, but often the debates have been more about the best questions to ask rather than about what the answers to particular questions are. (Sternberg 2020b: 3)

He then identifies and briefly discusses seven metaphors about intelligence he labels as geographic, computational, biological, epistemological, sociological, anthropological, and systems. He also considers mixed metaphors, and how they work in the study of intelligence.

Although he equates the word *metaphor* with the word *model*, he never tells us in this essay how he wants us to define either of these two words. He does say metaphors are like languages. "They are different ways of expressing ideas" (2020b: 14). At the risk of sounding more dismissive than we intend, what then is an idea? He ends his introduction simply saying this: "Sometimes, combining metaphors—even mixing them—is best of all" (2020b: 14).

We will not be debating in this book whether this is good advice. We will be considering, however, a number of popular models of intelligence (see Chapter 2). Then we will offer a model of our own (Chapter 3).

In this chapter, we want to build on Sternberg's observation that debating how to decide what intelligence is and isn't has often been about what are the best questions to ask rather than the best answers to give them. As scholars interested in human evolution, diversity, and our history as a species, we find it fascinating so many scholars say intelligence cannot be defined (Daley and Onwuegbuzie 2020; Kornharber 2020; Legg and Hutter 2007a, 207b; Sternberg 2020b), and yet this is something that:

1. can be measured,
2. varies from person to person, and
3. may vary, as well, from place to place on earth.

The issue, the question, therefore, at the center of this book is this one. Why should we believe any or all of these claims, these popular assumptions, and their sometimes dangerous implications?

Tools for Thought

The word intelligence is often used in ways assuming you know what it means. It is easy to get the impression, for example, that intelligence is something each of us has as one of our defining characteristics as a human being—one of our observable, or *categorical*, traits—similar to how tall you happen to be, or how fat you have become (Grigorenko and Burenkova 2020: 101). Is this true? Is intelligence an observable trait that can be used to describe and characterize you as a human being? Does it really make sense to say someone is not only short and fat, but also stupid? Or tall, slender, and brilliant?

In this book, we want to show you how this word can be redefined so it means something surprisingly obvious once you stop thinking of intelligence as a label for an elusive trait or characteristic like being fat or thin, wise or stupid. To do so, we are going to use a few visual tools—simple ways of picturing ideas—to "show," not just "tell about," what it takes for anyone—in fact, any creature with a brain—to survive, deal with life, and get what it can out of the time we each have on earth from the cradle to the grave.

1. Cartesian Graphs

Although we will not be using it often as a tool for thought, the first of these graphical aids is called a Cartesian coordinate system defined by two or more perpendicular axes plotted on a multidimensional plane. This

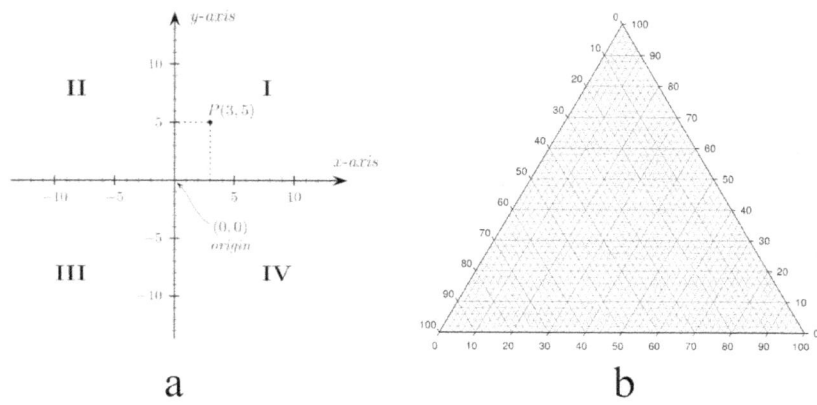

Figure 1.1. (a) A Cartesian coordinate system on a two-dimensional plane defined by two perpendicular axes. Gustavb, GNU Free Documentation License, CC BY-SA 3.0, via Wikimedia Commons. (b) Ternary plot. Tobias1984, CC BY-SA 3.0, via Wikimedia Commons.

kind of visual tool is a simple way to illustrate, for example, how two separate categorical traits, or characteristics, of something may somehow be linked—how they may be related. For example, how the size of something can be charted as a single point (labeled P3,5 in Figure 1.1a) measured at right angles to one another in two directions commonly referred to, say, as the dimensions called length and width.

What this type of graph does not show, however, is why these two dimensions are related because each can vary independently of the other. Technically speaking, the dimensions in a Cartesian graph are *orthogonal variables* (a piece of knowledge that only rarely comes up even in crossword puzzles). For example, you can be tall and thin, or tall and fat. But whatever the combination of traits, if you can count it, measure it, or weigh it, this kind of plot can be a good way to show how the traits or characteristics being studied may or may not be related to one another for one reason or another (Sundet et al. 2004).

2. Ternary Plots

The other type of visual tool is one we generally find more useful than Cartesian graphs. This type of diagram is called a ternary plot or graph, and sometimes a triangle plot (Figure 1.1b). These graphs are often used in the physical and earth sciences to show how three traits, or characteristics, rather than varying independently of one another (that is, separately), vary instead relative to one another. A simple down-to-earth example (pun intended) is a soil texture triangle showing how different kinds of soil can be classified as differing mixtures or combinations of sand, silt, and clay. Said another way, the kind of soil you have depends—note the word just used—on the mix of these basic types.

You might think that intelligence and soil have nothing in common, but we have found ternary plots to be a useful way to describe not only how things and events vary, but why all of us as human beings depend not simply on how our brains work as biological machines—what we will be calling in Chapter 3 the brain's *mechanical awareness*—but also on how the act of thinking itself unfolds as a give-and-take set of activities or abilities we see as working together on the *functional* and *relational* levels of intelligence.

We have a lot to say about these three levels of intelligence in this book, and we will be using ternary plots to help us do so.

Making Sense of Human Intelligence

The idea that intelligence is a personal trait like being short or tall, fat or thin, and so on is now firmly fixed in popular Euro-American opinion and psychological thought (Marks 2005). According to conventional wisdom, how we think can be fast or slow (Nettelbeck et al. 2020), right or wrong, logical or emotional, lazy or hardworking, intuitive or informed, and so on. What gets overlooked when we think in terms like these as elementary as A or B—as either/or possibilities, or dichotomies—is that intelligence, however defined, is broadly understood as the ability not just to react, but also to act.

Furthermore, being able to control what happens to us and around us largely depends on whether we have previously learned to deal with similar events and situations in the past. Hence not just agency but experience, too, are both critical to what generally would be seen as behaving intelligently.

Saying just this, however, is not enough. Both agency and being able to draw on what we have experienced in the past critically depend also on how well we are able to recognize similarities between what we already know based on past experiences and what we are dealing with in the here and now.

Therefore, instead of simply saying how intelligent you are—whatever we take this word to mean—is determined by how fast or slow, right or wrong, logical or emotional, and the like, you can be, it is critical to know:

1. What have been your past *experiences*?
2. How well can you *recognize* similarities between what you have already experienced and what is currently happening?
3. How have you already used what you have previously experienced to *explain* what is happening in the present?

Six Questions + 1

It has long been said there are six questions you should answer whenever you are reporting on a news story worth putting into print (or nowadays online): What? Where? When? Who? How? and Why? Although often neglected, there is also a seventh question to ask and try to answer: So What?

All seven of these questions can also be asked not just about the news of the day, but also about what the word intelligence means. The questions When? Where? and Who? are often asked about history and human evolution. We will not try to answer them in this book. The others—What? How? Why? and also So What?—are collectively, however, a useful way to sort through what has already been said and claimed about intelligence, whatever you take this word to mean.

There is no practical way to turn the questions What? How? and Why? into measurable features of the real world that might be labeled perhaps as "whatness," "howness," and "whyness" so they can be plotted together on a triangle graph. Even so, we have found that ternary plots are a useful way to envision the answers to these questions as the complementary dimensions of what it takes to end up with a balanced picture of what you are trying to understand and explain—rather than as measured independent orthogonal variables plotted in a multi-dimensional Cartesian space (Figure 1.2b).

What would be an example of the give-and-take relationships among the three reasons (popularly known as "causes") shown in Figure 1.2b? In a few words, natural means *what you can do*; necessary is *what you must do*; and invented refers to *what you decide to do* to achieve what you want to do. Therefore, one example would be learning what you need to know to become an innovative video-game developer with a high-paying job. Another, in the spirit of "practice makes perfect," would be dedicating a lot of your time and effort to becoming skillful enough to win at Wimbledon.

If much of everyday thinking can be labeled, as we have in Figure 1.2 as What? or CATEGORICAL thinking, and Why? or RELATIONAL thinking—your brain's way of trying to make sense of people, things, and events—then ternary plots or graphs like this one can be a useful way to

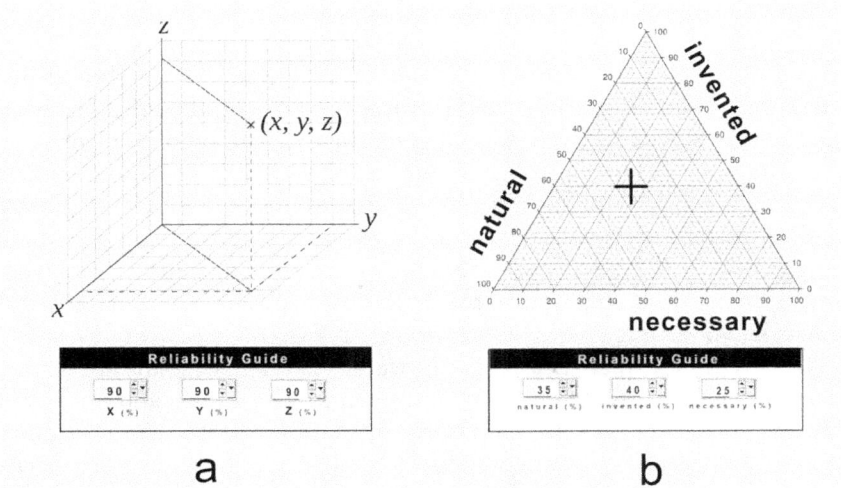

Figure 1.2. (a) Conventional everyday WHAT? or CATEGORICAL thinking is your brain's way of identifying what it may be dealing with in the world based on what it sees as the defining *traits, characteristics, elements, ingredients,* or *dimensions* (labeled here as X, Y, and Z) of what it takes to be different kinds, or "types," of things, events, people, etc. The *reliability* of what you are thinking is a *probability* between zero and 100 percent that you are right about each of these defining traits. For example, that the person who stole your backpack was not only male and blond, but also unusually tall. If you are wrong about any one of them, then the reliability of what you are thinking is directly affected. (b) WHY? or RELATIONAL thinking is your brain's way of trying to make sense of what it is experiencing, or might experience, by asking what could be the reasons, or causes (labeled here as natural, invented, and necessary), explaining such observations or results. While all of the possible reasons considered might be responsible, as the reliability guide shows, they may not all contribute equally to the observed or anticipated outcomes. © John Edward Terrell

show, not just tell, what you are trying to describe and understand. For example, instead of the words natural, necessary, and invented, you could substitute the words Earth, Sun, and greenhouse gases to write about why the cause or causes of climate change are both controversial and hard to pin down.

However, before we go on to see if we can pin down further what intelligence is all about, it makes sense to see how others have discussed intelligence in the past. Has intelligence always been considered to be a trait like being tall or being fat? If not, what can we learn from the past about how others have grappled with the problem of what it means to be able to think and act "intelligently"?

Conventional Answers

According to Robert Sternberg, people have often said we should just get rid of the word intelligence. However, he tells us, this idea has been around for a long time. Call it intelligence, discretion, scholastic aptitude, academic preparedness, or something else, he thinks this concept is likely to prevail whatever you elect to call it. "What Homer [in ancient Greece] believed to be a gift from heaven or a gift of the gods, today we would call a genetic gift. We merely attempt to express in a scientific way what Homer recognized well before the birth of Christ—that intelligence has at least some genetic (heritable) component" (Sternberg 2020c: 19).

As a credible explanation for why we are not all the same in all that we think and do, this statement would seem to be a truism and possibly a platitude. Offering such an observation seems comparable to the comical statement attributed to the comedian Groucho Marx: "Age is not a particularly interesting subject. Anyone can get old. All you have to do is live long enough." What Sternberg proposes seems to turn a good question— Why aren't we all the same in what we think and do?—into an answer similar to the claim that what makes us feel sleepy is something called a "somnolent factor." Or people do stupid things "because they are stupid." What have others, therefore, made of what is conventionally called intelligence?

René Descartes and the Soul

Western biblical traditions of our singular Creation in the Garden of Eden lead us to believe we are fundamentally not like other creatures on Earth. Instead, we are uniquely different. We are more than animals. We can think. We have souls. We can plan and plot. However, although often dismissed as "just folklore," not everybody always sees being human as something that is uniquely special and quite wonderful. In fact, not even in Europe has this self-serving haughtiness always been true.

Between the thirteenth and eighteenth century, for example, European legal history is rich in accounts of the criminal prosecution and execution of animals during which "the sentences were passed and executed in properly constituted courts of law by fully qualified magistrates, according to generally accepted laws" (Cohen 1986: 10). To offer one example: "In December 1457 the sow of Jehan Bailly of Savigny and her six piglets were caught in the act of killing the five-year-old Jehan Martin. All seven pigs were imprisoned for murder and brought to trial a month later before the seigneurial justice of Savigny" (1986: 10).

Figure 1.3. "Trial of a sow and pigs at Lavegny" in 1457. Robert Chambers (1869) *The Book of Days: A Miscellany of Popular Antiquities in Connection with the Calendar, Including Anecdote, Biography, & History, Curiosities of Literature and Oddities of Human Life and Character*, page 128: "Our artist has endeavoured to represent this scene; but we fear that his sense of the ludicrous has incapacitated him for giving it with the due solemnity." Public domain, via Wikimedia Commons.

Furthermore, as surprising as it may seem, according to the historian Esther Cohen different forms of execution were in use back then:

> Some of them closely paralleled the human precedent while others prescribed a peculiarly "animal" form of death. Thus in some places animals were dragged and hung like human murderers, while in others the authorities resorted to strangling or a knock on the head. The use of a tree instead of the "human" gallows was also occasionally apparent, though even then a proper hangman performed the job. Where the hangman's bills are extant, they closely resemble those presented for the execution of humans. (Cohen 1986: 12)

Sabina Magliocco at University of British Columbia has pointed out that folklorists have always had keen interest in animal lore. There are thousands of articles, books, and other sorts of publications on how humans have thought about and portrayed animals in their folklore. Recent research on animals "has illustrated that many of the distinctions we have drawn to separate ourselves from them—language, culture, self-awareness—in order to justify their instrumentalization and commodification, may well be arbitrary and wrong" (Magliocco 2018: 3). Some today would even argue the current willingness of the part of the behavioral and social sciences to "anthropomorphize" animals has reached a dangerous point, in part because, as the folklore scholars Brandon Barker and Daniel Povinelli have commented, studying animal cognition can be "maddeningly puzzling" (Barker 2019: 114).

Cohen has pointed out that the existence of such animal trials not all that long ago in Europe poses real problems for the historian. In Judaism and Christianity, we alone were created in God's own image to rule over Nature in His name. Hence the prosecution of animals runs counter to widely accepted understandings of justice, humanity, and the animal kingdom. Yet this practice survived in Europe and flourished for centuries (Cohen 1986: 15).

It is in this context that the famous words of the French philosopher René Descartes in 1637 seem oddly hard to place: *je pense, donc je suis*, "I think, therefore I am." This claim is one of the foundational ideas of modern Western philosophy, although this declaration is usually rendered not in French but rather in Latin as *cogito, ergo sum* (Holyoake and Morrison 2011).

To draw again on what Cohen has observed, European thinkers have done their best to find a clear boundary between us and beasts. "Perhaps the most extreme expression of this approach was Descartes's idea, that animals are automata possessing neither sense nor feelings. Within this framework it was inconceivable that a beast should be placed in a human situation and treated as a human being. Animal trials, however, did exactly that" (1986: 16).

Descartes accepted as a foregone conclusion that we alone have souls and are capable of rational thought (Hatfield 2007, 2017). Given this prior assumption, it seems self-evident that inside each of us there must be something—call it the "soul" if this sounds right to you—the dimensions of which may not be easily measured, but nonetheless can certainly be weighed. And when this happens, perhaps found wanting, too.

Descartes did not invent the concept of the soul, and he was not the first to grapple with the problem of how it is we are able to think about things that are not right there in front of us, to plot, to connive, and to wish even for unachievable rewards (Dennett 1988). It seems clear, however, that like those before and since, he was willing to attribute our awareness of the world around us and our responses to what we find out there to a singular, although immaterial, something that some would still call the "soul," and others might instead refer to as the "mind," the "brain," or the "intellect."

Sigmund Freud and the Psyche

In a benchmark essay published in 1999, the psychologist Eric Kandel observed that the great psychoanalyst Sigmund Freud revolutionized our understanding of the human mind during the first half of the twentieth century (Kandel 1999). Unfortunately, Kandel went on to say, during the second half of the last century, Freudian psychoanalysis did not evolve scientifically. It did not develop solid methods for testing and developing Freud's excitingly original ideas. As a consequence, Kandel gloomily concluded, psychoanalysis entered the current century with its influence in decline. He was not the first to declare Freud over and done with (Reisner 1999).

Much of the strength of Freud's way of thinking about how our brains work was unquestionably the richness of his portrayal of the human psyche. His trio of players on the private stage located between our ears—the *id*, the *ego*, and the *superego*—and the roles he had them play in shaping our actions, reactions, and psychological maladies had a completeness, a totality, about them that in Kandel's opinion no modern alternative school of psychology had yet matched.

Given Freud's prominence in the intellectual history of the last century, it may surprise you that nowhere in the 1,249 pages of the 50 chapters by 93 authors in the recent *Cambridge Handbook of Intelligence* (2020) is Freud mentioned at all. Similarly, he is not mentioned in the only chapter on psychiatry in the *Cambridge Handbook of the Imagination* (2020). Out of the 48 chapters in this collection by 68 authors, his name is invoked only in passing twice in a chapter offering a sociocultural perspective on current research on how we all draw on our own experiences, recombine them in various ways, and thereby come up with new alternatives and possible futures (Zittoun, Glăveanu, and Hawlina 2020).

This lack of attention to Freud by so many psychologists and other scholars writing about intelligence and creativity is surprising. In the quarter century since Kandel wrote about Freud and Freudian psychoanalysis, there have been prominent efforts by others to combine the analytical tools of modern neuroscience—notably, brain tissue imaging using functional magnetic resonance imaging (fMRI) and other technological advances—to promote what some are now calling neuropsychoanalysis (Cieri et al. 2023). As the philosopher Daniel Dennett has commented, however, whether updating Freud in the light of neuroscience is worth all the work involved is far from clear (Dennett 2020).

It would be hard to reject, nevertheless, what Freud did for our understanding of what it means to be human (Weston 1999). As Joel Weinberger and Valentina Stoycheva have written about in their book *The Unconscious: Theory, Research and Clinical Implications* (2020), he made us confront that most of what we do is driven more than many of us may like to accept by what our brains are doing without our knowing it. From an historical point of view, this was a revolutionary accomplishment.

Giftedness and Genetics

Writing about people called intellectually gifted for the *Cambridge Handbook of Intelligence*, Sally Reis and Joseph Renzulli at the University of Connecticut report that "there are no more varied groups of people than those labeled intellectually gifted." Undaunted, they are seeking answers to a number of basic questions including this one: "What combinations of genetic abilities and talents interact with one's personality and environment to produce intellectual giftedness?" (Reis and Renzulli 2020: 291).

As have many others, therefore, they evidently accept that an individual's biological ancestry is part of the reason why some people may be labeled as gifted, but others not. Yet they also report that "despite the label that this diverse population has been given, within the population some do and some do not demonstrate high levels of accomplishment in their education or their chosen professions and work." And furthermore, they go on to say that "scholars and researchers continue to debate definitions of giftedness, how intellectual giftedness develops, and the characteristics of diverse groups of high-potential youth that will help educators and psychologists to identify and nurture intellectual gifts and talents" (2020: 292).

What is notable about their commentary is that acknowledging how difficult it is to say who can be labeled as intellectually gifted has not discouraged these authors—and others—from using this label instead of simply rejecting it as impressionistic, even misleading. On the contrary, they report that since most contemporary researchers believe that IQ scores alone are inadequate measures of intellectual giftedness, "motivation, high self-concept, and creativity" are key qualities in addition to "intellectual potential" that must be taken into account (2020: 297, 308).

In short, the conviction that being intellectually gifted is somehow biological (and genetic) as well as learned (and cultivated) may be unshakeable: "Not surprisingly, within different cultures, contexts, and environments, the outcomes of intellectual giftedness vary. Cultural influences can negatively or positively affect the choices and products that emanate from one's gifts, and the ability to select, shape, and/or adapt one's environment" (2020: 297).

Therefore, instead of abandoning the concept, Reis and Renzulli accept that "a consensus has not and probably will not be reached about how to develop intellectual giftedness because of the very diversity of how we define giftedness. This lack of consensus may be completely appropriate, as the complexities surrounding this construct continue to both intrigue and challenge researchers" (2020: 308). Given this appraisal, what are the rest of us to think?

Nature or Nurture?

There is a school of thought in psychology called evolutionary psychology that insists much of what we humans do is figuratively speaking "written in our genes." Therefore, it is only natural to do things in a certain way because this is how they must be done (Smith 2020; see Figure 1.2). Practitioners of this view of ourselves as a species generally come down decidedly in favor of nature rather than nurture when it comes to understanding what is popularly talked about as "human nature."

However, as Daniel Kruger and his colleagues have remarked in a recently published survey, seeing things and events from an evolutionary perspective does not mean the same thing to everyone who looks at life this way. "There are, in fact, several topics researched under an evolutionary umbrella that are contentious or controversial, both within and outside the field" (Kruger, Fisher, and Salmon 2023: 11). As they go on to say:

> The relationship between nature and nurture in influencing behavior has been debated for centuries. And the question, which matters more, nature or nurture, is one discussed in every introduction to psychology course and textbooks. It is also a question debated by philosophers as well as lay-people when they question why someone turns out the way they do. Was it their parents? Their peers? Or was it their genes? (2023: 12)

The survey reported by Kruger and his colleagues Maryanne Fisher and Catherine Salmon had asked 581 professional scholars—who all see themselves as "evolutionary-informed researchers," and who were trained chiefly in psychology (58 percent), anthropology (18 percent), or biology (6 percent)—how they see evolutionary theory helping them understand human psychology and behavior. Nearly all of them (92 percent) agreed that nurture (described as "developmental environments") shapes adult human psychology and behavior in major ways. And yet a substantial majority (62 percent) also hold the view that the human brain houses separate "domain-specific, context-sensitive modules," and nearly all of them believe there are differences in human psychology and behavior based both on an individual's biologically defined sex (95 percent), and on their individual genetic endowment (93 percent). Furthermore, nearly three-quarters of participants agreed there are "population differences" resulting from "different ancestral ecologies and environments."

It seems clear these 581 scholars believe the issue they have been asked to consider cannot be reduced to an explanation as elementary as nature or nurture. They evidently all are willing to entertain the alternative that the resolve must be in the form of nature and nurture, not A or B, but instead A *and* B. However, what if the answer is more likely to be A, B, and C?

Consider this everyday example. Being aware of whether you are hungry may seem uncomplicated and decidedly biological, unquestionably about nature and (ironically) not nurture. Yet anyone who has ever tried to lose weight by dieting knows firsthand that habit and the time of day, or the smell of something truly delicious, can have a lot to do with feeling hungry. It is not just that your stomach is empty and cries out for something more. Yes, of course, biology has something to do with it. But so does what you have experienced in life. It is not surprising, therefore, that people often say that when it comes to nature or nurture, it is really both, not one or the other. In fact, not just both. It is now known that the microbes active in your gut can also weigh in on what and when you are keen to eat (Alcock et al. 2014: Stetka and Bomboland 2019).

Saying this, however, basically avoids explaining why this might be so. As Tom McAdams and his colleagues Rosa Cheesman and Yasmin Ahmadzadeh at King's College London have written about the confounding effects of sharing both genes and environments: "Parents are the source of both DNA and a rearing environment, and this makes it difficult to distinguish the effects of one from the other" (McAdams, Cheesman, and Ahmadzadeh 2022: 1). They have cautioned that even under ideal conditions, associations between biological characteristics (nature) and life experiences (nurture) are much like any other kind of association. Yes, they may be causal in nature, but they can also be spurious, inflated, or in other ways fundamentally misleading.

Therefore, in Chapter 3 and the Conclusion to this book, we are going to offer you a way of thinking about how we do what we do as human beings based on the biological realities of what it means to be human, but which sees these realities as foundational rather than deterministic (Jacob 1982: 65).

So What?

It is no secret that not everybody does everything equally well. With a little effort and thought, therefore, anyone can come up with a way to test people to pin down the sorts of things they are capable of doing at least reasonably well. Tests of ability are basic and routine, for example, when a football team is looking for new players, or when a symphony orchestra is auditioning new violinists or oboists.

It is also widely accepted that it is possible to measure how much of the "essence of intelligence" (Legg and Hutter 2007b: 393) you have been gifted biologically by your parents and more distant ancestors. Professional psychologists, too, have been confident in saying there is "a highly general mental ability with strong genetic roots that distinguishes among us in socially important ways" (Gottfriedsen 2003: 392). Nearly a decade earlier, the same scholar had been even more forceful in an editorial in the *Wall Street Journal* in 1994: "IQ is strongly related, probably more so than any other single measurable human trait, to many important educational, occupational, economic, and social outcomes" (Gottfriedsen 1997: 14).

The standard measures of intelligence still in use are IQ (Intelligence Quotient) tests that are descended directly, or by inspiration, from the test invented by the French psychologist and educator Alfred Binet in the early twentieth century. Binet himself was aware that an individual's performance on these tests is heavily conditioned by their experiences in life and the physical and social environment they live in (Marks 2005: 215). When IQ testing came to the United States, however, Lewis Terman at Stanford University almost single-handedly became one of America's leading advocates for using intelligence testing to identify unusually skillful thinkers. Unlike Binet, Terman believed heredity has a lot to do with how brilliant you are.

Testing for Intelligence

At the turn of this century, *Stanford Magazine* took a backward look to the days in the previous century when Terman was a towering figure at the university there in California, one of Stanford's first really big campus stars. Under the diplomatic title "The Vexing Legacy of Lewis Terman," Mitchell Leslie, the author of this popular piece, notes that Terman believed his "genius study" of kids with high IQs had "established a powerful new research approach: the longitudinal investigation, in which scientists follow a group of people over many years to learn how factors in early life influence later variables such as health and longevity" (Leslie 2000). All to the good, but then Leslie tells us this about Dr. Terman:

A story of a different kind emerges from Terman's own writings— a disturbing tale of the beliefs of a pioneer in psychology. Lewis Terman was a loving mentor, yes, but his ardent promotion of the gifted few was grounded in a cold-blooded, elitist ideology. Especially in the early years of his career, he was a proponent of eugenics, a social movement aiming to improve the human "breed" by perpetuating certain allegedly inherited traits and eliminating others. While championing the intelligent, he pushed for the forced sterilization of thousands of "feebleminded" Americans. Later in life, Terman backed away from eugenics, but he never publicly recanted his beliefs.

Self-fulfilling Prophecy?

Anyone can come up with a test to try to prove that something they want to call intelligence truly exists. Since nobody knows for sure what this word means, however, this is a tough assignment. What does it tell us about someone, for example, if they are good at answering typical IQ questions such as the following? What number should come next: 54, 49, 44, ___? Which two words mean the same thing?—*fugacious, vapid, fractious, querulous, extemporaneous*. What is the missing pattern in Figure 1.4?

Steven Rose, a neuroscientist and biologist—and a founding member of the British Society for Social Responsibility in Science—observed some years ago: ". . . IQ is clearly a flexible construct—as amply demonstrated by decisions in the 1930s and 1940s in the United States and Britain to 'adjust' test questions to equalize the scores of boys and girls, because in previous versions of the tests girls had scored higher" (Rosen 2009: 787). Perhaps the most obvious thing, however, about using IQ tests to measure something called intelligence is how similar the test-maker and test-taker need to be culturally and linguistically (Flynn 2007, 2020; Richardson 2012: 595). As the biological anthropologist Jonathan Marks has bluntly stated: "if the subjects do not share the same assumptions as the researchers, and are not motivated in precisely the same manner as the designers of the tests and the initial subjects, they will not score as well" (Marks 2005: 216).

Nonetheless, it has been routine in the U.S., and in some other countries, too, to give IQ tests to immigrants who speak little or no English. This has often resulted in astonishing low IQ scores leading to the impression that foreigners are likely to be mentally inferior. Based on Gene Anderson's own research work and enquiries, for instance, this was the case until recently in New York State and California. Fortunately, New York State in recent decades has used the results of intelligence testing to place the resulting "failures" in classes teaching English as a second language rather than in homes for the "feebleminded."

Figure 1.4. An example of a visual IQ test question used to measure what is said to be general human intelligence and abstract reasoning, User: Life of Riley, CC BY-SA 3.0, via Wikimedia Commons.

To make measuring intelligence an even more daunting assignment, it has also often been claimed, and disputed, that intelligence is not just one thing, but a number of different things—*language intelligence, logical and mathematical intelligence, spatial intelligence*, and so forth (Kornhaber 2020). At the same time, it is often claimed that even if this diversity of intelligences is real, nonetheless, there is also still something called the "g" factor (as in *general intelligence, general mental ability*, or *general intelligence factor*) that intelligence testing can uncover explaining something like half or so of what makes us smart, or not so smart, depending on your biological (genetics) heritage (Walrath et al. 2020).

The Secret Ingredient?

In a way reminiscent of the role that a hypothetical substance called *phlogiston* played centuries ago in now outdated alchemical theories of combustion (Figure 1.5), what we have written about in this chapter shows that it has not been necessary to define intelligence to accept that this is somehow the vital ingredient—nowadays many would still say the special biological ("genetic") ingredient (Grigorenko and Burenkova 2020:

Figure 1.5. An alchemist in his laboratory. Conrad Gessner (1599), *The practise of the new and old phisicke, wherein is contained the most excellent secrets of phisicke and philosophie, deuided into foure bookes*, London, Peter Short. Before the discovery of the chemical element oxygen at the end of the eighteenth century, it was widely believed that there was a fire-like element called *phlogiston* inside combustible materials that was released when they burned. (As an aside, Gessner is generally also credited with the invention of the pencil.) Public Domain Mark, via Wellcome Collection.

101)—inside each of us that somehow makes some of us special and better than the rest of us in some favored way.

In this chapter, we have surveyed briefly how several well-known thinkers and writers in the past tried to explain why it is that all of us seem to differ from one another far more than in other species not only in our physical appearance, but also in our behavior. For reasons that are not always apparent (and are not always kind, or helpful), judging how well or poorly those of our own kind are able to do something some of us believe to be special, rare, and wonderful might even be said to be one of the defining characteristics of our own species.

This desire to explain our obvious diversity has led to the claim of long standing that there must be something inside each of us variously called the *soul*, the *ego* (along with the *id* and the *superego*), or *intelligence*, that determines how well we are able to get through life and make a success of ourselves.

Although nobody seems to be able to agree on how to define intelligence, there is a common thread running through many of the attempts to do so. The core issue often seems to be this one: *How well can you solve a problem?*

Here then is one way to think about intelligence we have found useful. In keeping with the conviction that a good answer to any complex question is not going to be as simple as "it's just black or white," "this or that," or even "A and B," ask yourself these three questions when you want to know how someone is likely to deal with life's demands:

1. Can they *see* the problem?
2. Can they *solve* the problem?
3. Did they *create* the problem?

We suspect this third question may surprise you. Does this question sound somehow off-key? We do not think so, but explaining why we include it here will have to wait until the last chapter in this book.

Right now, we want to give you a quiz. The three questions just asked lead to three ways to define what the word intelligence means. Which of the following definitions do you think we have in mind (check one or more)?

- being effective
- being aware
- being delusional

In the next chapter, we will continue to survey what this word has been taken to mean by many for years, but instead of looking inside the human body to find there a secret ingredient like phlogiston making us either truly gifted or only run of the mill, we will be considering how four famous scholars have sought to find the answer not inside the human body, but outside in the environment, in the world we all must deal with from the cradle to the grave.

Key Points

1. People are not all equally as skillful in all that they do, say, or think.
2. Explaining why this is so by claiming some people are far more intelligent than other people turns a good question—if we all belong to the same biological species, why are we not all the same?—into an answer explaining nothing about why we aren't all alike.
3. The belief that there is something called intelligence hidden inside each of us that can be measured using standardized IQ (Intelligence Quotient) tests—and which somehow makes some of us special and better than the rest of us in some favored way—has historically been used to extend privileges to some and discriminate, harm, and even kill others of our kind.

2

Possible Answers

Although there is no agreement today on the meaning of the word *intelligence*, what four well-known scholars have written about learning, socialization, and decision-making shows there is, nonetheless, a common theme. Intelligence is often said to be about how *effectively* we deal with the world outside our skulls.

Ever since the Russian scientist Ivan Pavlov in the last century made public his pioneering experiments on how animals—most famously dogs—learn when dinner is served and other basic facts of life, laboratory researchers have been trying to pin down the inner secrets of intelligence, both human and "other" (Tully 1973). As we discussed in Chapter 1, an enduring mystery about being human is how much of what we are able to do is written in our genes before birth, and how much we must learn—like Pavlov's dogs—from our own personal and social experiences first as babies and children, and then as fully grown adults. We are convinced, however, and others have been, too, that this is not the best way to think about this mystery commonly referred to as the "nature or nurture debate."

The Logic of Simple Words

According to the conventional wisdom of many around the world, being intelligent means not just thinking rationally but also logically. As defined by the *Cambridge Dictionary*, the word *logic* refers to "a particular way of thinking, especially one that is reasonable and based on good judgment." This definition, however, leaves much to be desired even after looking up how the same dictionary defines "thinking," "reasonable," and "judgment." When other information sources are also consulted, you learn that to be logical, something needs to be correct, valid, true, and reliable. It is an understatement to say this is asking a lot.

Without pretending, therefore, to be logicians of world standing, we have found that it makes sense to avoid using the simple logic of the little word "or," and opt instead in favor of the equally simple word "and." Rather than assuming, however, that the best answers are likely to be A and B, we lean instead toward answers like A, B, and C or A, B, C, and D, and so forth. Take, for example, what the Nobel Laureate Jacques Monod wrote half a century ago.

Chance, Necessity, and Choice

Chance and Necessity (*Le Hasard et la Nécessité*) is a best-selling book by the biochemist and World War II hero Jacques Monod (Carroll 2013). He lays out chapter by chapter how the story of life on earth has been an ever-changing dialogue between the senseless "chance" creation of purely random biological variation at the molecular level, and the absolute "necessity" of repeating over and over again via reproduction, sexual or otherwise, what has been written in the DNA recipe for life called the genome. Why is this important? Because no single organism lives forever. What has been "written in our genes" is vital practical and historical information encoded in every genome that must be reproduced, generation after generation, for the very survival of life on earth.

There is more to life, however, than merely repeating from one generation to the next what has already been recorded in our genes about what to do to stay alive. What is in our genes may be the "cards" we have been given biologically to play the game of life with, but how we play these cards also leads not only to our own personal success, but also what we are able to pass on to future generations. Moreover, as Monod emphasizes, we are not the only creatures that can constructively play the cards they have been given by their forerunners:

> Animals, and not only those nearest us on the evolutionary scale, unquestionably possess a brain capable not just of retaining and recording pieces of information but also of associating and transforming them, of bringing the result of these operations back out in the form of an individual performance; yet not—and this is the essential point—in a form which permits the communication to another individual of an original, personal association or transformation. But this is what can be done with human language, which may be considered by definition to have been born on the day when creative combinations—*new* associations achieved by one person—by reason of their transmission to others no longer had to perish with [the person who invented them]. (1972: 129; also 155)

What Monod is saying here, at least in this English translation of his French text, could perhaps be said more easily some other way, but what he is referring to is what in the social sciences is called *agency*. He is saying that agency is not just a characteristic of our own species (1972: 149). Other animals, too, have agency even if, lacking our capacity for using (and misusing) language, they cannot easily communicate to others what they have learned about how to make the most and more of what they have been given biologically through their genes to work with. Therefore, Monod tells us, and we agree with him, understanding how and why things are the way they are is not just a tale about blind chance and absolute necessity (1972: 154–55). Often it is also about agency—about making choices and acting creatively.

If this is so, then how skillful and effective—many would say how intelligent—anyone happens to be clearly cannot be reduced to the A or B logic of nature vs. nurture. How clever, how smart, we are at any given moment for any given reason depends not only on chance and necessity, but also on choice. Therefore, intelligence, however defined, needs to be seen as a combination of at least all three. Whatever this combination is taken to be, if it could somehow be measured or weighed, it must be something located somewhere within the triangle of a graph formed by all three (Figure 2.1). Exactly where on such a ternary plot, of course, would depend on how influential each happens to be in determining what someone is thinking, saying, or doing.

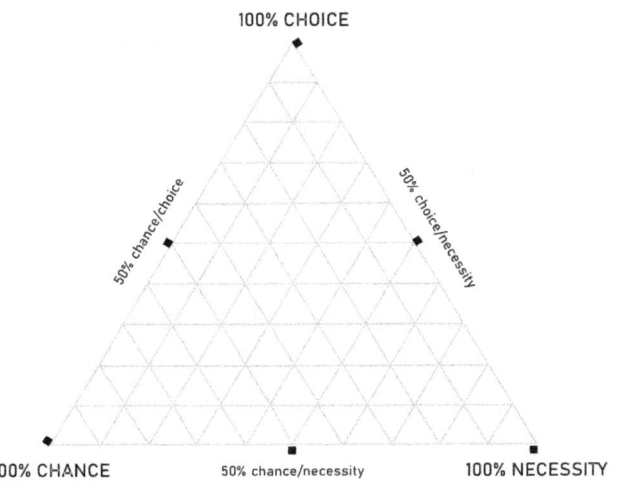

Figure 2.1. Understanding how and why things are the way they are at any given time calls for weighing the roles not only of chance and necessity but also choice. © John Edward Terrell

The Blind Men and the Elephant

Even if you disagree with what we have just said, and favor instead solutions to the riddle of what makes us human as simple as nature or nurture, it is obvious we do not all do everything equally well. Four renowned scholars during the twentieth century, two of whom were Nobel Prize recipients in economics, wrote extensively about how our experiences rather than our genes can determine how good we are at being clever, rational, and skillful about what we think, say, and do. Looking back at what they wrote, we find that how they tackled the elusive issue of intelligence brings to mind the famous Indian parable of the "Blind Men and the Elephant."

There are many versions of this tale. They differ most notably in how many blind men are said to be touching the same (or as some versions say, different) elephants. The common thread running through them is that seeing the Truth is harder to do than most of us may want to believe. Here is a version by the influential Hindu scholar and religious leader Râmakrishna Paramahansa (1836–1886) telling us the world's many religions are each only partial truths about enlightenment, and that "He alone who has seen God in all His aspects can settle all disputes" (Râmakrishna 1907: 28–29):

> Four blind men went to see an elephant. One touched a leg of the elephant and said: "The elephant is like a pillar." The second touched the trunk and said: "The elephant is like a thick club." The third touched the belly and said: "The elephant is like a huge jar." The fourth touched the ears and said: "The elephant is like a big winnowing-basket." Then they began to dispute among themselves as to the figure of the elephant. A passer-by, seeing them thus quarreling, asked them what it was about. They told him everything and begged him to settle the dispute. The man replied: "None of you has seen the elephant. The elephant is not like a pillar, its legs are like pillars. It is not like a big water-jar, its belly is like a water-jar. It is not like a winnowing-basket, its ears are like winnowing-baskets. It is not like a stout club, its trunk is like a club. The elephant is like the combination of all these." In the same manner do those sectarians quarrel who have seen only one aspect of the Deity. He alone who has seen God in all His aspects can settle all disputes.

Unlike the passer-by in this old fable, we will not be saying that these four scholars have each told us something wrong about being intelligent, rational, and wise. Moreover, they have all taken the biological side of each and every one of us more or less for granted. They have all tried instead to deduce what it is that makes us human from what they see in how we all respond to life's challenges.

Table 2.1. All four of these famous scholars have interpreted intelligence to mean how effectively someone is able to achieve their goals. Both Simon and Kahneman, who were awarded the Sveriges Riksbank Prize in Economic Sciences in Memory of Alfred Nobel for their work, have described our success at making our own choices in life as one of the hallmarks of our evolutionary success as a species. © John Edward Terrell

What we can think and do according to:	Skinner	Geertz	Simon	Kahneman
Is determined by . . .	our environment	our social environment	what we are able to learn about our environment	how hard we work to figure things out

Like the blind men in the tale, each of these four has done so insightfully in his own way. B. F. Skinner compares us to the pigeons in his laboratory. Herbert Simon sees us as behaving like ants wandering across a beach. Clifford Geertz says we would be lost and basically incompetent without the guidance and help of others. Daniel Kahneman says we are being lazy when we do not try to arrive at the best answers to life's challenges and demands.

There is much to be gained by knowing what they have written about being human. Yet each has denied or largely ignored something fundamental about what makes us what and who we are. It's not biology or genetics. Here is a hint: we have just called it *choice*. Also in the background of what they have written is an equally fundamental question: *What makes us all so diverse as human beings in our ways and thoughts?*

B. F. Skinner and Behaviorism

> "There is no place in a scientific analysis of behavior for a mind or self."
> —Burrhus Frederic (B. F.) Skinner (1990)

Burrhus Frederic Skinner was famously opposed to "mentalistic explanations" for human behavior. By this he meant giving the brain a decisive role in determining how we behave. In his eyes, trying to explain what we do by appealing to inner states of mind, feelings, and other elements of an "autonomous man" inside our skulls is unscientific and a waste of time. "The ease with which mentalistic explanations can be invented on the spot is perhaps the best gauge of how little attention we should pay to them" (Skinner 1971: 160). He had no patience for anyone saying we do what we do because we have intentions, purposes, or goals in mind, or something as intangible as "free will" (Skinner 1977). As he describes Freud and psychotherapy in his influential textbook *Science and Human Behavior*:

> Unfortunately, he chose to represent the relationships he discovered with an elaborate set of explanatory fictions. He characterized the ego, superego, and id as inhabitants of a psychic or mental world subdivided into regions of conscious, co-conscious, and unconscious mind. He divided among these personalities a certain amount of psychic energy, which flowed from one to the other in a sort of hydraulic system. (Skinner 1953: 375).

Skinner saw himself as a scientist seeking demonstrable truths, not fanciful ideas. The "task of a scientific analysis is to explain how the behavior of a person as a physical system is related to the conditions under which the human species evolved and the conditions under which that individual lives" (1971: 14). Said even more directly, "the fact remains that it is the environment which acts upon the perceiving person, not the perceiving person who acts upon the environment" (1971: 188).

What he meant was that how we behave is controlled—or as he would say it, "conditioned"—by how often and how rewarding what we are doing proves to be. A classic example would be laboratory mice or pigeons learning they will receive a food pellet as a reward when they press a lever in their cage. Or if someone says something witty and everyone in the room laughs, they may be inclined to say the same thing at another time and place, too.

Skinner conceded the reality of what he described as the "indisputable fact of privacy." This suggests he knew he could not get away with claiming people do not have their own opinions and inner thoughts. Even so, he stuck to his environmental determinism. "It is always the environment which builds the behavior with which problems are solved, even when the problems are to be found in the private world inside the skin" (1971: 195).

He had a hard time convincing everyone he was right. In a review of his 1971 book *Beyond Freedom and Dignity*, the linguist Noam Chomsky scathingly rejected Skinner's claims. "His speculations are devoid of scientific content and do not even hint at general outlines of a possible science of human behavior. Furthermore, Skinner imposes certain arbitrary limitations on scientific research which virtually guarantee continued failure" (Chomsky 1971; also Chomsky 1959). Other reviews of this book have been as dismissive.

Skinner often invoked biological evolution and Darwinian natural selection when arguing for his point of view as the true and proper way to study why we do what we do as human beings (Skinner 1981, 1990). His staunch behavioral approach to psychology left no room for the brain of any animal doing anything of much interest or direct relevance between receiving the input of an environmental stimulus (for example, Ivan Pavlov's bell telling his laboratory dogs their food had arrived) and an animal's response (in Ivan's case, his dogs salivating in anticipation of their next meal).

Skinner's self-confidence in the correctness of his way of analyzing human and animal behavior is frankly hard to understand. What is the point of having a brain, and in particular a brain as big as a human brain, if it has basically nothing to do? He loved to invoke Darwin and natural selection, but what would be the beneficial consequences of evolution favoring anything more costly to run than the elemental nervous system of a clam or an oyster?

Perhaps even more puzzling is why he evidently felt that the challenges of life are so predictable and elemental that chance, not just choice, has no role to play in what Darwin called the struggle for existence while apparently being comfortable with claiming that, for example: "People do not observe particular practices in order that the group will be more likely to survive; they observe them because groups which induced their members to do so survived and transmitted them" (1981: 503). It is just naive and foolish, therefore, to believe even for a moment that we can act on our own behalf or for the greater good of others. As he wrote in 1981: "We tend to regard ourselves as initiating agents only because we know or remember so little about our genetic and environmental histories" (1981: 504).

Hence the mystery behind the work of B. F. Skinner is real enough (Overskeid 2007). Why did he not see that people have the big brains they have because we are not just living in the past? We have them because we must cope with the challenges—and seize the opportunities—that living in the here and now not only impose upon us, but offer us, too? That is, if we can seize the day and make what we can of what life gives us? He had much to say about *how* we learn, but basically took a pass on dealing with what and why.

Skinner appears to have been so focused on how he could control the behavior of pigeons, people, and other living creatures that he may have overlooked a likely possibility. Yes, of course, how "positive" or "negative" we find our experiences to be may influence how likely we are to repeat—he would say "respond with"—a similar sequence of actions based on what we have previously done in more or less the same situation (some would call this "blind faith"). But does an experience really need to be positive or negative? Isn't it more likely that it is simply the *repetition* of an experience that strengthens the *memory traces* involved (Holler et al. 2021)? There is a good word in English for this likelihood. It's called *learning*.

Clifford Geertz and Cultural Symbols

> In sum, human intellection, in the specific sense of directive reasoning, depends upon the manipulation of certain kinds of cultural resources in such a manner as to produce (discover, select) environmental stimuli needed—for whatever purpose—by the organism; it is a search for information.
>
> —Clifford Geertz (1973)

Clifford Geertz was one of the leading theorists of twentieth century social anthropology. He saw the task of the ethnographer as interpreting what he called cultural symbols—"words for the most part but also gestures, drawings, musical sounds, mechanical devices like clocks, or natural objects like jewels—anything, in fact, . . . used to impose meaning upon experience" (Geertz 1973: 45). He is famous for describing the scholarly work involved as "thick description," and for saying that being an ethnographer means dealing with "a multiplicity of complex conceptual structures, many of them superimposed upon or knotted into one another, which are at once strange, irregular, and inexplicit, and which he must contrive somehow first to grasp and then to render" (1973: 10).

Some anthropologists today consider his characterization of what it takes to understand our human ways and customs as a license to project their own freewheeling interpretations on other people's behavior, but Geertz had no patience with this view. "I have never been impressed by the argument that, as complete objectivity is impossible in these matters (as, of course, it is), one might as well let one's sentiments run loose. . . . [This] is like saying that as a perfectly aseptic environment is impossible, one might as well conduct surgery in a sewer" (1973: 30). He insisted instead on the importance of checking our scholarly interpretations carefully against local views. With this in mind, he also focused his own professional work on public matters: language, ceremonies, politics, expressive culture, and the arts. Still, his scholarship has been criticized both by other social anthropologists and those in the cultures he himself described for being too imaginative.

Like the word *intelligence* in psychology, what social scientists take the word *culture* to mean has long been, and still is, much debated. Defined as learned behavior shared by those in social groups, Geertz accepted that culture seen in this way basically shapes all human intellectual life and experience. For him (as for many anthropologists trained in the last century), how we think and even what we think about is socially acquired. We all are, therefore, mostly the products of our upbringing, not the creations of the genes we have inherited from our parents and more distant ancestors. Consequently, "man is an animal suspended in webs of significance he himself has spun, I take culture to be those webs, and the analysis of it to be therefore not an experimental science in search of law but an interpretive one in search of meaning" (1973: 5).

> ... there is no such thing as a human nature independent of culture. Men without culture would not be the clever savages of Golding's *Lord of the Flies* thrown back upon the cruel wisdom of their animal instincts; nor would they be the nature's noblemen of Enlightenment primitivism or even, as classical anthropological theory would imply, intrinsically talented apes who had somehow failed to find themselves. They would be unworkable monstrosities with very few useful instincts, fewer recognizable sentiments, and no intellect: mental basket cases. As our central nervous system—and most particularly its crowning curse and glory, the neocortex—grew up in great part in interaction with culture, it is incapable of directing our behavior or organizing our experience without the guidance provided by systems of significant symbols. (1973: 49)

This view of what it means to be human gives us little room either for innate physical responses, or for individual originality and expression. In his eyes, our emotions and even our physical needs are shaped by the symbols we learn from others. Yes, we can be original and creative now and then, but only within socially prescribed ways and within culturally constructed forms.

This way of seeing what makes us human strikes us as too blinkered, too narrow, and too limited. Yes, it makes sense to see symbols as socially learned ways of finding patterning and repetition in things and events happening around us. But such perceived patterns do not have to be socially prescribed and interpreted by publicly recognized symbols to be meaningful or instructive.

Thus, for Skinner, we all are just another kind of animal, possibly smarter than pigeons, but we learn and think in the same animal ways. For Geertz, each individual is instead a representative, a living example, of a specific cultural tradition. Skinner neglected the questions *What?* and *Why?*, and made much of the question *How?* Geertz took the latter question to be about social learning, and the *Why?* question to be about needing to be told by others who already knew how to survive and make it through life. What interested him most was the *What?* question: what is the guidance we are thankfully "provided by systems of significant symbols?"

Herbert Simon and Bounded Rationality

> Human beings, viewed as behaving systems, are quite simple. The apparent complexity of our behavior over time is largely a reflection of the complexity of the environment in which we find ourselves.
>
> —Herbert Simon (1996)

Herbert Simon had much to say about the human brain's decision-making skills and the role of rationality in the conduct of human affairs. He repeatedly acknowledged in his writings that the words "rational" and "rationality" are tricky ones. Economists, for example, have long had a heroic picture of the human mind. "Classical economics depicts humankind, individually and collectively, as solving immensely complex problems of optimizing the allocation of resources. The artfulness of the economic actors enables them to make the very best adaptations in their environments to their wants and needs" (Simon 1996: 49).

This view of what it means to be human seems about as far removed from Skinner's austere behaviorism as you can go. However, Simon argued that this conventional understanding of what it means to be rational demands far too much of the human brain. Given all that we would need to know to be able to make the best choices—which he took to be the most "rational" ones—the most any of us can do, even with our highly capable brains, is look for the most satisfying answers for solutions to life's challenges that are bound to be, at best, just "good enough" and sufficiently rewarding when it comes to deciding what to do in life.

Furthermore, but still unlike Skinner and other behaviorists, Simon saw what he called "the outer world," the environment, as setting the terms and conditions for success, but not our goals and decisions in life. Said simply, for Simon, being intelligent means behaving rationally, and behaving rational, means adapting your actions to fit your circumstances so that you can achieve your goals as best you can (Simon 1978).

Therefore, the strength of what he proposed as an alternative to behaviorism is that he tells us we are thoughtful creatures intent on achieving our goals by adjusting our actions to fit our opportunities. This is so even if what we end up doing falls short of being the most rational, the most capable, the most logical of all possible solutions to life's problems. Three challenges to this rosy view of life, however, are easily overlooked.

First, Simon says that as a species, we are skilled at reworking the world around us to meet our needs, goals, and desires. Consequently, we can make the world we live in less risky and uncertain than it otherwise would be. On the face of it, being able to do this is both wise and rational. Often, too, this may be true. But not always, given the two other limitations.

Second, people do not always have the same goals and desires. When disagreements arise, conflicts and tragedies can result (Simon 1996: 43–44). This fact about being human is perhaps most obvious in the great diversity of languages, customs, and even desires around the world. Hence there is much about the world—some would even say "worlds"—we have created for ourselves that is not just self-made, but also arbitrary and diverse. Simon often used the word *artificial* to describe such unnatural human creations. Unfortunately, there is nothing necessarily "rational" about being self-made, artificial, arbitrary, and diverse.

The third limitation we see in Simon's way of thinking about intelligence and being human is how similar he seems to B. F. Skinner in what he wrote about our bounded rationality and our seemingly advanced ways of figuring things out for ourselves. Here is one of his often-quoted observations: "Analogous to the role played by natural selection in evolutionary biology is the role played by rationality in the sciences of human behavior" (1996: 8). It is hard to credit why he would say this is so.

Charles Darwin's theory of evolution by means of natural selection views all life on earth as caught up in a constant and competitive struggle for existence. Moreover, as most evolutionists today insist, Darwinian evolution is *not* insightful. Biological evolution does not have goals. It does not have purposes. There are no "shoulds" in evolution. So why would Simon want us to accept that our bounded rationality and natural selection have much in common?

Early in his highly successful book *The Sciences of the Artificial*, Simon tells us that "an ant, viewed as a behaving system, is quite simple. The apparent complexity of its behavior over time is largely a reflection of the complexity of the environment in which it finds itself." Shortly thereafter, he goes on to substitute "human being" for the word ant:

> A thinking human being is an adaptive system; men's goals define the interface between their inner and outer environments, including in the latter their memory stores. To the extent that they are effectively adaptive, their behavior will reflect characteristics largely of the outer environment (in the light of their goals) and will reveal only a few limiting properties of the inner environment of the physiological machinery that enables a person to think. (1996: 53)

We think Skinner himself could not have said this more eloquently. Ironically, Simon here both acknowledges our human capacity to be inventive and at least in some ways rational—to create artificial worlds of our own design—and yet evidently does not see that rationality and artificiality are not just synonyms for the same thing.

Daniel Kahneman and Heuristics

> Much of the discussion in this book is about biases of intuition. However, the focus on error does not denigrate human intelligence, any more than the attention to diseases in medical texts denies good health. Most of us are healthy most of the time, and most of our judgments and actions are appropriate most of the time.
>
> —Daniel Kahneman (2011)

In the 1970s, Daniel Kahneman and his late colleague Amos Tversky carved out a professional niche as experts on the many ways in which we all make mistakes when we use mental shortcuts and simplifying assumptions leading us to believe things we really shouldn't (Kahneman and Tversky 1973, 1979; Kahneman, Slovic, and Tversky 1982). They popularized calling such mentally quick and dirty thinking tactics "heuristics and biases." Heuristics are simple shortcuts; biases are oversimplifications that lead to specific kinds of factual distortions (Berthet and de Gardelle 2023).

A good example of what they and others have called heuristic shortcuts is the *fundamental attribution error*: the fallacy of thinking that a quality or feature of something you commonly see must be something changeless about that kind of thing (Kahneman et al. 1982). This type of faulty thinking easily leads to error, especially in how we see other people. Yes, a rock is always hard, trees are always woody, and water always flows downhill. But these simple truths do not mean that someone who is shy in one kind of situation is always shy everywhere, and hence can be labeled a "shy person." Or someone who is often talkative and outgoing always behaves this way and never feels awkward and shy.

Another common type of heuristic error, or fallacy, is the tendency for all of us to polarize differences into simple dichotomies (A or B) and ignore intermediate states—to see things as black and white, rather than in shades of gray.

These and other familiar weaknesses of our human grip on reality are explored in detail in Kahneman's best-selling book, *Thinking, Fast and Slow* (2011). How can such basic misjudgments and mistakes be explained? What is it about how we deal with the world that leads to such errors of judgment and choice? Kahneman and others argue that all of us are capable of thinking in two differing ways (Evans and Stanovich 2013). One way is fast and simple. The other is slow and more cautiously reasoned.

Fast thinking—commonly called *System 1* or *Type 1*—is done rapidly without much effort, and happens more or less subconsciously. For example, when you notice a motion out of the corner of your eye, but do not react to it. Or when we talk without thinking about whether we are sticking to the rules of good grammar. Speakers of English, for instance, know it is OK to say "the nice big green wooden house," but not "the wooden green big nice house." Nobody deliberately really needs to teach anyone this basic grammar, and children rarely think about it consciously as they learn how to talk and start to share their inner thoughts and wants with others.

Slow thinking, also called *System 2* or *Type 2*, is thinking that is more intentional, harder to do (more "effortful"), slower, and hence is more "costly" (thinking this way uses greater amounts of your body's metabolic energy). For example, when you are self-consciously trying to remember where to use the pluperfect subjunctive in Spanish (even native speakers of Spanish have trouble with this). Consequently, slow thinking is likely to be more accurate and reliable than fast thinking—although not always. Or at any rate, so Kahneman and others have argued.

One of his examples of System 1 thinking is what is initially called for to drive a car on an empty road (2011: 21). As traffic thickens, a veteran driver does not suddenly shift to System 2. She gets slowly more and more aware of the traffic around her, more and more attentive, and more and more self-consciously cautious. Her conversation with her passengers usually does not immediately stop. Instead, what she has to say gets more and more perfunctory until the traffic gets potentially dangerous. Then she is likely to stop talking entirely. When this happens, her passengers are just as likely to be aware of what is going on, and they also shut up.

Kahneman argues that most of the time when dealing with the world, we use System 1. Doing so also lets us focus on things we really want to do and may need to use System 2 to do. Technically often called the "dual-process model" of how we think, this current labeling revives, and applies in new ways, the old idea that there are two ways to think about things: rapid intuition and cautious deliberation.

What does all this have to do with intelligence as an assumed phenomenon? Although he makes little of it, Kahneman seems to have accepted that intelligence has a biological basis, even if he never tells us in *Thinking, Fast and Slow* what this might be. Here, for example, is what he says there about where intelligence fits into the picture of how fast or slow we are thinking about things and events:

> As you become skilled in a task, its demand for energy diminishes. Studies of the brain have shown that the pattern of activity associated with an action changes as skill increases, with fewer brain regions involved. Talent has similar effects. Highly intelligent individuals need less effort to solve the same problems, as indicated by both pupil size and brain activity. A general "law of least effort" applies to cognitive as

well as physical exertion. The law asserts that if there are several ways of achieving the same goal, people will eventually gravitate to the least demanding course of action. In the economy of action, effort is a cost, and the acquisition of skill is driven by the balance of benefits and costs. Laziness is built deep into our nature. (2011: 35)

Others have argued that the heuristic strategies and biases favored by System 1 thinking are more useful for their shortcut value than in their metabolic cost savings. Gerd Gigerenzer, in particular, has shown that taking the easy course of action only rarely leads to major mistakes (Gigerenzer 2007; Gigerenzer et al. 1999). Gigerenzer also points out that it would be impossible to get by in life living by slow thinking alone. Just watch a baby learning to walk—if she had to think consciously and seriously about every step, she would not get far. Therefore, he argues, our species has evolved a workable compromise between System 1 and System 2 that maximizes efficiency while reducing errors.

The word intelligent occurs 26 times in *Thinking, Fast and Slow*, and intelligence is used 29 times. Both are employed in ways assuming there is something special about intelligence, and that people who can be called highly intelligent have inherited their ability to be that way (2011: 46, 401). It is revealing, however, that he also uses the word lazy 15 times. While he clearly sees intelligent people as being less prone to making silly mistakes and System 1 errors, he also argues that all of us can fall victim to the seductive appeal of thinking fast when we ought to be thinking slow. Why? Because "System 2 is lazy, and that mental effort is aversive" (2011: 64).

It is also telling that the words rational, rationality, and the like occur in this book well over 130 times. It is not difficult to see where Kahneman wants our species to be, even if we are not there yet, and evolution has a lot of work to do before we can claim to be truly rational creatures. Labeling, however, being anything other than cautious, careful, and deliberate as being "lazy" may sound perfectly appropriate, but saying this ignores the limitations of what in this book we are calling "mechanical awareness"—about which we have a lot to say in the next chapter.

A One-Sided View of the Human Nature

We have only briefly discussed what these four scholars have written about learning, intelligence, and the human mind. What we have noted may be enough, however, to show how they have accepted the traditional wisdom that how intelligent people happen to be depends on how well—how effectively—the brain "interacts with environmental challenges"

(Jung 2020: 549). Perhaps the most obvious difference among what these experts have proposed lies in how active or passive people are when they are learning and using what they need to know to survive and prosper.

1. B. F. Skinner most emphatically saw learning as a passive process (Figure 2.2a) during which the lasting impact of what is being learned is strengthened through repetition. What he left largely unexplained is how and why such meaningful repetition occurs. Simply stated, who or what in real life (rather than in the psychologist's laboratory) is controlling the conditions favoring learning is left unspecified and evidently taken for granted.
2. Clifford Geertz similarly saw learning as mostly a passive process (Figure 2.2b), but unlike Skinner, he was unequivocal in telling us who is teaching us how to behave. Rather than having to discover solutions to life's challenges on our own, those who already know how to behave teach us what to do and how to do it. What we are taught by others does not turn us into mindless robots. Instead, what we learn socially is "a set of control mechanisms—plans, recipes, rules, instructions (what computer engineers call 'programs')—for the governing of behavior" (1973: 44). He favored calling these control mechanisms "symbols." He wrote confidently that without "organized systems of significant symbols—man's behavior would be virtually ungovernable, a mere chaos of pointless acts and exploding emotions, his experience virtually shapeless. Culture, the accumulated totality of such patterns, is not just an ornament of human existence but—the principal basis of its specificity—an essential condition for it" (1973: 46)
3. Unlike Skinner and Geertz, Herbert Simon portrayed behaving intelligently more directly as an active but flawed decision-making process (Figure 2.2c). As creatures, he argued, who are incapable of dealing fully with the world in all its complexity, we form simplified pictures of the world and its challenges (Simon 1980, 1996: 44). Furthermore, like Geertz, Herbert Simon insisted that from "birth until death, our ability to reach our goals, even to survive, is tightly linked to our social interactions with others in our society" (1996: 154). However, to repeat what we noted earlier, our goals in life define the interface between our inner and outer environments. Our behavior, therefore, largely reflects characteristics of the outer environment, and reveals only "a few limiting properties of the inner environment of the physiological machinery that enables a person to think" (1996: 53).

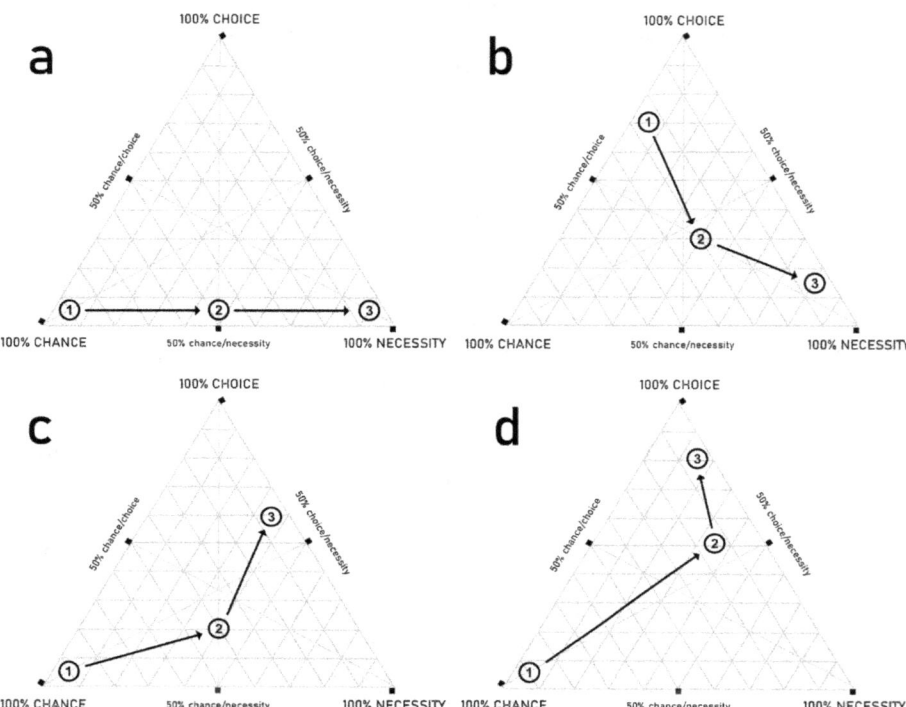

Figure 2.2. How variable or predictable we end up being [3] in how we behave differs according to the four famous scholars we have discussed in this chapter. (a) For B F. Skinner and other behavioral psychologists, the likelihood that what we do will be repeated depends on whether what we have done has been positively or negatively reinforced (rewarded), and not on whether we chose to do what happened. (b) Clifford Geertz, on the other hand, grants us the freedom to decide what to do, but even so, we must be taught by others how to behave properly and well. (c) In contrast, Herbert Simon grants that we can make choices in life, but he assumes the choices we make are ones reflecting the demands and opportunities of the world around us. (d) Like Simon, Daniel Kahneman insists that how intelligent we are reveals how rational we are—how closely attuned we are to things and events outside the limits of our skulls. But more so than Simon, he cautions that good answers to life's questions may take more work than we may want to invest in being successful. © John Edward Terrell

4. Like Simon, Daniel Kahneman has described being able to make accurate and effective decisions about what to do and why as the hallmarks of being intelligent (Figure 2.2d), a state of mind he defines not only as "the ability to reason; it is also the ability to find relevant material in memory and to deploy attention when needed" (2011: 46). Perhaps less like Simon, however, he has described being rational as an active but easily misleading decision-making process. Although for both, how rational we are depends in part on how well we can find ways to do what needs to be done "at some specified level" of success (Simon 1956: 136), Kahneman seems more inclined to warn us about being intellectually lazy: "Those who avoid the sin of intellectual sloth could be called 'engaged.' They are more alert, more intellectually active, less willing to be satisfied with superficially attractive answers, more skeptical about their intuitions. The psychologist Keith Stanovich would call them more rational" (2011: 46).

In summary, therefore, it can be seen from what these four scholars have written that intelligence is commonly taken to be about how effective we are as individuals and (some would add) as groups, or supposed "kinds" of people, in dealing with the external world and its ways from the cradle to the grave. If this is what intelligence is all about, however, does this mean thinking about things for any other reason is a waste of time and maybe even stupid? Or is this traditional point of view literally too one-sided?

Is There a Better Answer?

In Chapter 1, we considered some of the many claims advanced over the past few centuries for thinking there must be something real, although elusive, inside each and every one of us that naturally determines in advance how successful and competitive we can be in life. In this chapter, we have discussed instead what might be called the other side of the same coin, the side conventionally called nurture.

Although it may come across as too obvious to need saying, there is a difference between whether you can, and whether you do. The claim there is something inside each of us that governs how well we can do something with our lives can be taken as a blameless excuse for not being as wise and wonderful as we would like to think we are. On the other hand, those who favor nurture over nature have a job to do when it comes to justifying why we aren't perfect in word and deed, a concern that Kahneman has written so firmly about.

Despite their different concerns and conclusions, all four of the famous scholars selected here out of the many we could have written about have taken nature more or less for granted. Yes, of course, how we are endowed by biology, genetics, and ancestry surely has something to do with how we behave and what we can accomplish. But they have asked instead, each in his own way, how the challenges we face as we live our lives shape the outcomes of what we end up doing.

Like the passer-by in the fable about the blind men and the elephant, we are convinced, however, that taking "nature" for granted so you can see why things happen on the "nurture" side of life doesn't work. Doing so means you end up seeing only one side of the "elephant" that has long been the object of dispute called "nature or nurture?" (Jacob 1982: 61–62). In the next chapter, therefore, we map out for you how we think it is possible to see both nature and nurture working together to enable us to do not just what we have to do to survive, but also—and frankly too easily—make mistakes in life that, on calm reflection, are all too human and sometimes disastrous.

Key Points

1. All four of the scholars we have surveyed in this chapter have accepted the traditional wisdom that how intelligent you are depends on how well—how effectively—you are able to deal with the world around us. Perhaps the most obvious difference among what these experts have proposed lies in how active or passive you are when you are trying to survive, prosper, and achieve your goals, whatever they may be.
2. What is "in our genes" may be the "cards" we have been biologically given to play the game of life with, but how we play those cards contributes not only to our own personal success, but also what we are able to pass along to future generations.
3. If this is what intelligence is all about, however, does this mean thinking about things for any other reason is a waste of time and maybe even stupid? Or is this traditional understanding of something (whatever this is taken to be) called intelligence literally too one-sided?
4. Although it may come across as too obvious to need saying, there is a difference between whether you can, and whether you do.

3

INTELLIGENCE REDEFINED

Deciding how smart someone may be by judging how fast or how well they are able to do something ignores how all of us make mistakes and sometimes think unlikely thoughts. Instead of saying intelligence is something we all have to a greater or lesser degree, it is useful to think about what it means to be intelligent as the interplay, or balance, among three basic cognitive skills or talents: *awareness*, *recognition*, and *imagination*.

What it means to be human has long been questionable and often debated. From a traditional Western biblical perspective, for example, we were all created in God's own image to rule over the rest of creation in accordance with His commands. The downside, however, of our exalted role in God's eyes is that we are not only able to think for ourselves, but we can also think sinful thoughts, thereby risking His displeasure and eternal punishment.

On the other hand, as discussed in Chapter 2, twentieth-century behavioral psychologists saw little merit in our alleged ability to think either for ourselves or about much of anything, for that matter. In their eyes, we are little more than biologically constructed robots capable of responding to what life throws at us mostly in uncreative ways derived more or less solely from what we have already experienced in life. From this narrow and nearsighted perspective, spontaneity, creativity, and free will are all basically shams and delusions.

Nowadays these extreme views may not be as widely acceptable as they once were. This does not mean, however, that there is agreement on how our human ways of thinking and behaving can be best characterized and understood. Building on ideas discussed previously (Terrell 2014; Terrell and Terrell 2020), we want to suggest an unconventional way of thinking about intelligence and why we sometimes make mistakes. This strategy looks not so much at how thinking goes on, neurologically speaking, up there in our skulls (Dehaene 2014; Graziano 2019). Instead, it builds on what are the limitations, constraints, and rewards of what we are able to know and think about ourselves and the world around us.

The Allegory of the Sleeping Dogs

The expression "let sleeping dogs lie" has been an idiom in the English language for centuries. Some see its origin in an Old Testament biblical proverb about not grabbing a stray dog by the ears (Proverbs 26:17). This traditional saying is commonly taken to mean "leave well enough alone," or "don't go looking for trouble." The assumption at the heart of such an idiom is that a dog may attack you if you risk suddenly waking it up. Perhaps. But always? Certainly not the dogs we know. However, the fact that the dogs in question are sleeping is evidently also to be seen in itself as unremarkable. After all, isn't this what dogs often do?

According to the *Cambridge Dictionary*, a parable is a story about an idea, particularly a moral or religious one. Turning this saying about sleeping dogs into a parable like "The Blind Men and the Elephant" (see Chapter 2) is more than we feel confident we can handle. Moreover, what we have in mind is neither moral nor religious. However, according to the same dictionary, an *allegory* is "a story, play, poem, picture, or other work in which the characters and events represent particular qualities or ideas that relate to morals, religion, or politics."

Coupled with the picture of sleeping dogs shown here, we think the lesson in this old idiom is that—despite the claim that evolution is all about the survival of the fittest in the constant global struggle for existence—even dogs living on the street can apparently feel comfortable enough about life that they feel more than merely comfortable about taking a nap when and wherever they have a mind to do so. Yet even more telling perhaps, they evidently can do so when major street protests by human beings are taking place not far away in Taksim Gezi Park in the historic city of Istanbul, Turkey. Therefore, yes, life may be hard and sometimes dangerous, but even dogs, and certainly also people, clearly have a say in what they do, and whether they want to do it.

What then is the lesson we draw from this alternative take on the old advice about letting sleeping dogs lie? There really is more to life than the struggle for existence. Regardless whether you are talking about people, dogs, or any other kind of creature with a brain, do not assume what they are doing is not something they have chosen to do, however reasonable or wrong it may be to do it.

> ### Allegory of the Sleeping Dogs
>
>
>
> Despite the claim that evolution is all about the struggle for existence, even dogs living on the street feel comfortable enough about life to take a nap when and wherever they have a mind to do so. They can even do so when major street protests by human beings are taking place not far away in Taksim Gezi Park in the historic city of Istanbul, Turkey. Life may be hard and sometimes dangerous, but even dogs, and certainly also people, have a say in what they do, and whether they want to do it, however wise or wrongheaded it may be to do so.
>
> Dogs sleeping in Istanbul during the Taksim Gezi Park protests, 2013. Image taken by John Lubbock, Jwslubbock, CC BY-SA 3.0, via Wikimedia Commons.

The choices we make in life may not always be earthshaking, but they can sometimes be disastrous. It is hard (we would say impossible) to read the minds of others, human or other. But what about ourselves? How do each of us make the decisions we make? What decides how wise, foolish, or inconsequential they may be? If "wise" is just a shorter word for "intelligence," what does it take to be wise, and how difficult is it to be smart?

Dogs, Descartes, and Alan Turing

Anyone who has or has ever had a dog, a cat, or some other family pet knows firsthand what our allegory of the sleeping dogs is trying to convey. In Chapter 1, when we were discussing the seventeenth-century French philosopher René Descartes, we underscored how he had tried to get around the question of whether animals can think by declaring that they cannot because they do not have souls. In his eyes, animals are just self-operating robots, automata having neither feelings nor good sense. We alone have souls. We alone are capable of being rational.

This dismissive claim may well be what Descartes believed. We are confident most pet owners would be surprised to hear this is what he wanted us to believe, too. Even if he was right that pets do not have souls (many nowadays would say neither do we), to claim they cannot think, and cannot also connive and plot, would surely come across to them, as it does to us, not only as misinformed but ignorant.

Why is this important? At least as early as 1941, the mathematician Alan Turing was thinking about machine intelligence—what is now more commonly called Artificial Intelligence (AI). The opening sentence of his now famous paper "Computing Machinery and Intelligence" in the journal *Mind* in 1950 reads: "I propose to consider the question, 'Can machines think?'"

He quickly goes on to turn this question into a game he calls the "imitation game" (Turing 1950: 433). Put simply, can you tell whether you are dealing with a person or with a clever computer when you are doing so remotely? If you can't—and it is a computer you are dealing with—then that computer wins. And by winning, Turing argued, it has demonstrated to us that it is just as intelligent as we are.

Today, nearly three-quarters of a century later, what Turing had only imagined back then is now looking more sinister than just a game. With the arrival of chatbot software that lets us talk to computers as if they were people, for example, teachers are having to decide if they can detect whether the written assignments turned in by their students have been composed by them, or by a computer (Floridi and Chiriatti 2020).

Even if talking to computers is not something you like to do, what does losing to a computer mean? Pet owners may be right that their pets are at least somewhat intelligent. Machines may fool us into believing they are just as intelligent as we are. But what does a machine being as intelligent as we are really tell us either about computers, or about ourselves and how intelligent we happen to be (Biever 2023; Damassino and Novelli 2020)?

Intelligence, Neuroscience, and Brain Mechanics

The claim that intelligence can be defined as a general mental ability for reasoning, problem solving, and learning is often used to argue that intelligence can be reliably measured by standardized tests capable of predicting "several broad social outcomes such as educational achievement, job performance, health, and longevity." Therefore, some say "a detailed understanding of the brain mechanisms underlying this general mental ability could provide significant individual and societal benefits" (Colom et al. 2010: 489).

Given such confidence in how well IQ testing can predict individual and social outcomes, it seems ironic that modern neuroscience methods of brain scanning are commonly used to support conclusions about the brain resembling those advanced back in the nineteenth century (Figure 3.1; Jasanoff 2018: 17–18, 83–90). That was when the pseudoscience of

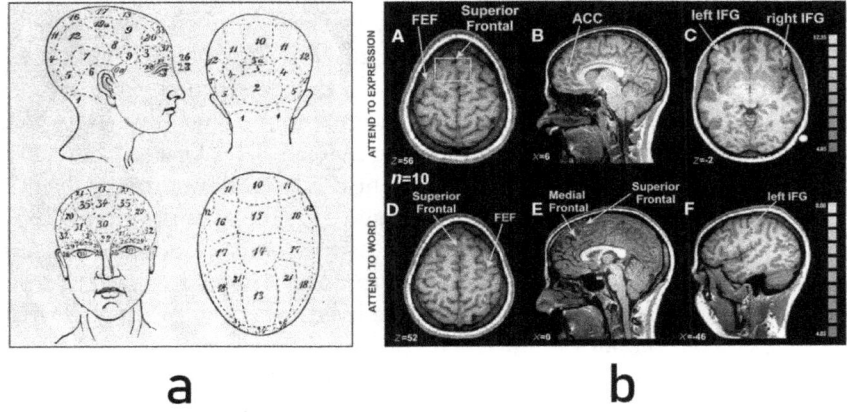

Figure 3.1. (a) Phrenological chart, *Webster's Academic Dictionary*, circa 1895. Public domain, via Wikimedia Commons. (b) Different brain structures involved in the recognition of a word and an emotional expression observed using functional MRI. Gray-tone adaptation, Shima Ovaysikia, Khalid A. Tahir, Jason L. Chan, and Joseph F. X. DeSouza, CC BY 2.5, via Wikimedia Commons.

phrenology was claiming you could predict a person's mental traits by observing the size and shape of bumps on the outside of their head (Jones et al. 2018; Satel and Lilienfeld 2014). Nowadays, it is again being said that different "brain functions"—according to some researchers, possibly more than 60 different "abilities" such as language, memory, learning, visual perception, information processing, knowledge, and so forth—are located in different parts of the brain inside our skulls (Colom et al. 2010: 491, and their fig. 4).

Skeptics are not reluctant to suggest that perhaps the most obvious difference between what was once being claimed long ago and what is now being proposed today in neuroscience is obviously not that there are separate regions of your brain doing different things for you, but that these functionally specialized areas of gray matter inside your skull are now thought to "interact and influence each other in a massive, resonating network" (Graziano 2019: 84). Given this understanding of how a brain works its magic, the "principle behind neural networks is that each neuron is extremely simple, but when they are connected together in large numbers, they are capable of great computational power" (Graziano 2019: 140–43; Jasanoff 2018).

According to some scholars, therefore and perhaps not surprisingly, high levels of intelligence as a general mental ability (measured using standardized IQ tests such as the Wechsler Adult Intelligence Scale) are thought to be traceable to "more efficient parallel information transfer" using these neural networks connecting these many apparently differentiated brain areas (Colom et al. 2010: 497). But how can anyone measure something that isn't a thing in itself (what the philosopher Immanuel Kant called the *Ding an sich*, literally the "thing in itself"), but instead a bunch of many functionally different things somehow all wired together?

Robert Sternberg remarked decades ago that the assumption more intelligent people are "rapid information processors" underlies most tests used to identify the gifted, including both creativity tests as well as those said to be measuring intelligence. But in his estimation: "What is critical is not speed per se, but rather, speed selection—knowing when to perform at what rate and being able to function rapidly or slowly depending upon task or situational demands" (Sternberg 1984: 282). Daniel Kahneman would surely agree (see Chapter 2).

Therefore, instead of thinking of intelligence as a kind of wiring in the brain (Pulvermüller 2023), we think it makes more sense to talk about how the human brain navigates its way through life as a set of three interrelated talents or abilities even if we cannot assure you that these talents are lodged safely away in different places inside your bony and possibly somewhat bumpy head.

Awareness, Recognition, and Imagination

At the start of this book, we proposed that rather than saying some people are smart and others are stupid, or some are wise and others foolish, it makes sense to talk about how the human brain works as a mix of three interrelated mental talents: *awareness*, *recognition*, and *imagination*. Using these three dimensions of what it means to think, our goal in this chapter is to show you why all of us are not as smart as we may think we are. Why not? Because of how we all learn about, recall, and try to understand the world we live in. Our hope is that knowing this may make it easier for all of us to work against our inherent weaknesses—and thereby live up to the scientific label Linnaeus gave us, *Homo sapiens*.

Awareness

Thinking comes so naturally to us as human beings that we may not realize it is much harder to do than we are likely to believe. As defined at the start of Chapter 1, being intelligent commonly means being able to learn, understand, and make judgments or have opinions based on reason.

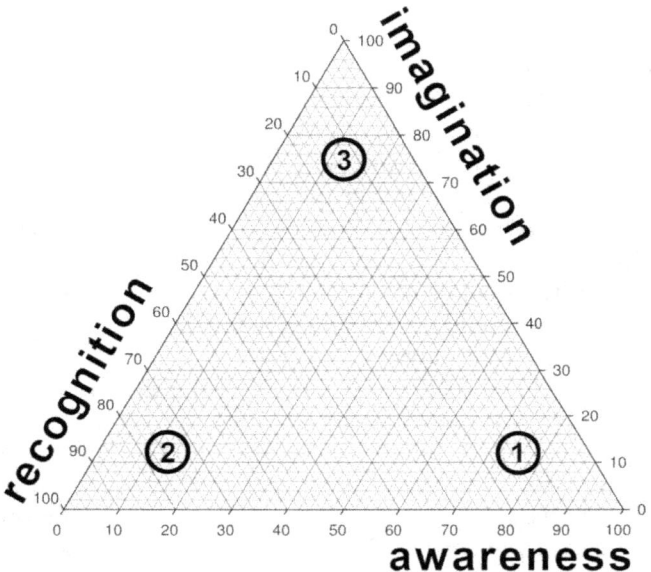

Figure 3.2. Three basic abilities of the human brain when you are dealing with the world around you (and also with your own aches and pains). (1) Attending to what is going on is a balance between awareness, recognition, and imagination in which attending to things and events outside your skull dominates. (2) Converting your bodily sensations into useful information by connecting them with what you already know through your previous experiences. (3) Trying to make sense of what is evidently happening or could happen. These three mental functions are sometimes conscious, but not necessarily so. Moreover, in different situations, we rely on these three neurological talents in different ways. For example, when we are daydreaming, we dial down how aware we are of what is happening around us. Some might say these three are different and distinct "cognitive modules" (Bolhuis et al. 2011), but in reality, no one knows how these functions are performed by the brain. It is more than likely that they can be done more or less simultaneously, although not necessarily all with an equal commitment of your brain's resources. For further discussion, see: Terrell and Terrell 2020. © John Edward Terrell

Furthermore, reason does not just mean having an excuse or explanation for an event or situation. The mental ability to reason means being able "to make a particular judgment after you have thought about the facts of a situation in an intelligent and sensible way."

However useful dictionary definitions such as these may be, they make it sound as if everyone understands what the other words used in these definitions mean and what they are all about. For example, that "the facts of a situation" are both knowable and already known. If true, then we simply have to put them together correctly and in a nicely logical way to be intelligent and rational. Perhaps, but how likely is this to be true?

John's Physics teacher in high school many years ago liked to say to his students "the obvious is seldom seen" (above, Introduction). Since they were trying to master basic principles of electricity and magnetism, and understand what on Earth (and in the Universe) are the laws of motion, gravity, and thermodynamics, John does not recall they ever asked him to explain why he would say this as often as he did. Psychology back then was still working in the shadow of Sigmund Freud and B. F. Skinner. Therefore, maybe even he could not explain why the human brain might behave in such a seemingly foolish way.

Our guess would be that he was mostly basing the wisdom encoded in this catchy remark on two common observations about how people can stumble when they are dealing with the world around them. One of these is how easy it is for all of us to "miss the point" of what someone else is telling us when we are not listening carefully enough. The other one is how easy it is even when we are aware of what we are doing to "make mistakes" now and then—and not just because we are either very young and inexperienced, or very old and frail.

Simply defined, therefore, awareness of something means having knowledge or perception of a situation or fact. Reality, however, is complex. What is it that determines whether we are aware of something, consciously or unconsciously, "out there" or "going on" around us? Awareness is not about something we have, but instead about something we do that can be seen as contingent on—depends on—successfully completing four conditional steps: *exposure*, *perception*, *experience*, and *recognition*.

1. Exposure

Hearsay testimony by a witness about what someone else evidently saw or experienced is not often allowed as incriminating evidence in a court of law. Such is rarely the case, however, in everyday life, and for a good reason. Life for all of us is complex enough that it is not possible to be always in the right place at the right time to experience things and events directly for ourselves. We have to rely mostly on what we learn from others through word of mouth, social media, letters, books, and so forth. Yes, as the popular saying goes, "facts matter." Yet if being intelligent means thinking "about the facts of a situation in an intelligent and sensible way," then there is no escaping the basic fact that most often we must take what are "the facts" we need to think about as a matter of faith, not firsthand experience (Hemmatian and Sloman 2018).

This is the first handicap of being intelligent individuals. We cannot always simply "think for ourselves." Furthermore, learning socially from others of our kind is not something only human beings do (Zentall 2020). Ironically, by this criterion alone, since we must rely so heavily on hearsay rather than on our own personal experiences as we navigate our way through life, other animals—since they cannot rely as strongly as we do on verbal communication with others of their kind—might be ranked, as surprising as this may sound, as more intelligent than we are (Holland 2024)!

Moreover, the fact that we can communicate with others by words as well as deeds means we can also far more easily be led astray. Now that chatbot computer programs using artificial intelligence (AI) and natural language processing (NLP) are able to talk directly to us when they are responding to our questions and concerns, whether what we are being told is true or false may be even harder to discover. No mistake about it, when facts matter, verbal communication can be more of a disability than a blessing.

2. Perception

It is no secret that much is going on, and always has gone on, in the Universe and down here on Earth that we are unaware of—at least not without the help of tools designed to extend the scope of our bodily senses and overcome our inherent sensual deficiencies. Nowadays what would we do without stethoscopes, microscopes, telescopes, surveillance satellites, radar detectors, security cameras, and the like? The wonder is not that people once believed the Earth is flat, or that the Sun goes around us day in and day out. It is only astonishing that anyone would now believe such nonsense, even if some still do. Yet until Nicholas Copernicus and other skeptics came along in the 1500s to argue that the Earth and the Planets visible up there in the sky revolved around the Sun, nearly everyone had accepted for thousands of years that the Earth is unquestionably seated at the center of all things in the Universe. But is this surprising? After all, we all know that appearances can be deceiving.

The notion that the Earth is flat or that we are living at the center of the Universe are both classic examples of the common enough human failing of seeing things solely from our own point of view. Yet who doesn't know from their own firsthand experiences that seeing things solely in this way can be grounds not only for heated arguments, but can also lead us to make otherwise avoidable mistakes that may get us into genuine difficulties.

Being self-centered in this way, however, is not the only reason for saying we all are not as clever and intelligently informed as we might want to

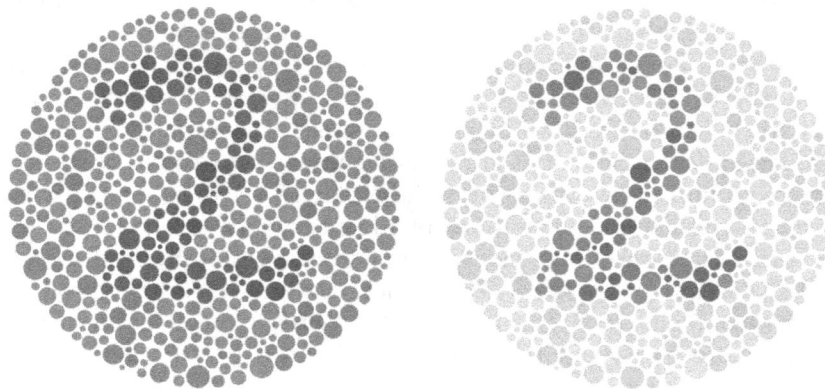

Figure 3.3. A gray-tone version of an Ishihara color test panel (numeral 2 in pale green on pink dotted background). The Ishihara color test for detecting red-green vision deficiencies is named after its inventor Dr. Shinobu Ishihara at the University of Tokyo, who first published his tests in 1917. It is a well-recognized fact that the real world does not have the colors our eyes tell us are "out there" to be seen, and not all of us "see" the same colors. Sakurambo, CC BY-SA 3.0, via Wikimedia Commons.

believe we are on the now entrenched assumption that we are surely the brightest creatures on Earth. For instance, it is a well-recognized fact that the real world does not have the colors our eyes tell us are "out there" to be seen, and furthermore, we are only able to see what our eyes are physically capable of seeing.

What this means, briefly noted, is that they can only detect electromagnetic radiation in the wavelengths that are visible to us, which are those generally in the frequency range between 380 to 700 nanometers. Other wavelengths are too large or too small and energetic to be visible to us. These limitations may seem trivial, but they have profound implications for how well we can learn what is happening around us, and thereby perhaps anticipate what will be the likely consequences down the road of what is going on from moment to moment in the here and now.

Furthermore, there is no need to argue the fact that the size of something and how far away it happens to be also makes a difference in how well, or even whether, we are aware of things and events going on around us. The world we can know directly without the aid of microscopes, telescopes, and the like is limited to things and events that are intermediate between those that are too remote, too attenuated, or too protracted to be noticed, and those that are too small, too dense, or too rapidly occurring to be sensed—to be perceived—without using specialized tools designed specifically for the purpose.

3. Experience

Common sense tells us things we should not take to be true. For example, that the world as we experience it is identical to the world as it truly exists, and if we are not simply delusional, we can be reliable witnesses to what is actually going on "out there" beyond our skin and bones. Therefore, if we simply pay enough attention to what is happening around us, there is a good chance our personal experiences will mirror reality more or less faithfully. Or so it is commonly said. Given what we have just written about *exposure* and *perception*, there is ample reason to doubt what common sense says.

Now that computers, cell phones, and the like are so much a part of daily life for many of us, it is also often claimed that our brains are able to take in via our senses something called "information" that already exists out there in the real world, "process" it, and then "store it away" in the form of something conventionally called "memories" that can be later "retrieved" and "restored" to something called our "consciousness" (Epstein 2016). This optimistic and largely passive view of what your brain does to help you get through life safe and sound may make sense to a computer scientist and perhaps also many cognitive psychologists nowadays (Gigerenzer 2020), but this mechanistic view of how and why we know what we know about life and the world around us is more imaginative than realistic.

Said simply, the sensations transmitted to our brains by our nervous systems do not start off as something called information. Far from it. Although there is much debate about how it does so, there is wide agreement that your brain plays a major role in determining what you end up making of the signals your body's biological sensors are picking up and sending along for your brain to intercept, interpret, and then somehow either store away for later use, or discard (Felin, Koenderink, and Krueger 2017; Koch 2019: 16–17).

Consequently, how well your brain becomes involved in what you know about the world around you can play a major, even a decisive, role in determining how well you end up handling what life throws at you. Despite what behaviorists in the last century may have preached, and to use a word now favored in the social sciences, both conventional wisdom and neuroscience nowadays concur that our brains can engage in something called *agency*, a word that the *Cambridge Dictionary*—and other dictionaries, too—defines as "the ability to take action or to choose what action to take."

Furthermore, although what they are and how they work is biologically and psychologically debatable, it is clear that what are called *emotions* and *feelings* can dramatically impact, too, how aware we are of what is going on around us (Jasanoff 2018: 101–3, 135). How we react to what we are experiencing can significantly influence not just how aware we are of things and events, but also how likely we are to remember what we are experiencing.

Although what is happening up there on your shoulders when you are tracking what is going on around you (and inside you, too) is poorly known and much debated (Blackmore 2020; Graziano 2020), our awareness of the world and inner selves is so much a product of what the human brain does with the sensations it receives that it is more than simply fanciful to say it is a kind of biologically constructed virtual reality device. The difference, of course, is that the sensations you experience through a virtual reality headset, however realistic they seem, are not really "out there" to be experienced.

4. Recognition

Much of our awareness of the world around us is only passive, and we have little conscious sense that we are in any way monitoring what is going on around us near and far. When we are actively aware, however, of what is happening in the outside world, our sense of things and events can be detailed, vibrant, emotional, and constantly changing. These facts are real clues as to why the human brain is not a camera or video recorder. As big as the human brain is, it would quickly run out of somewhere to save the accumulating trillions of momentary images. As Wim de Neys (2021: 9) has remarked: "we are always surrounded by gazillion potential stimuli. Sound, light, and pressure waves constantly hit our retinas, ear drums, and skin. Only a fraction of these are consciously perceived and attended." While nobody knows for sure how it is done, when our experiences become turned into memories, it is not every frame of the "reality video" you are witnessing that gets saved for later use. Instead, what may somehow be committed to memory "after the fact" is *just the most salient and constant features* of what is being picked up by your senses (Graziano 2019: 99; Seth 2021).

If this sounds unlikely to you, try drawing something you see everyday when it is not visible, say, the view outside your window, or a banknote. Then draw the same thing as best you can "from life" when it is right there in front of you. Far more than just nine times out of ten, your first drawing will at most possibly resemble what you had in mind, but that is about all. And it is not just a question of artistic skill. Even successful artists need to jump back and forth time and time again from seeing something to portraying it. It is not just a matter of how talented you are; it is also a matter of how limited your brain is when you are performing such a task.

The benefits of being able to remember, consciously or not, that even just a little bit about the world around us and what is happening in it are obvious to anyone who has ever had to master, say, finding a door in the dark (Zlomuzica and Dere 2022: 2). Yet here again is another limitation on how intelligent we all can be. For any given task or challenging problem, it is not a foregone conclusion that we have already learned enough of the right stuff to respond effectively and well. This is why your parents and teachers scolded you for not paying attention to what they were showing and telling you.

Furthermore, conventional wisdom tells us that the habits and assumptions we develop over time are different from the memories we acquire as we live our lives. Habits and assumptions are said to be things we believe and do without having to think about them. Memories are thoughts and recollections we can retrieve and consciously relive—such as what a specific flower is called, or where you put your glasses when you took them off to wash your face. It may be comforting to believe this supposed difference makes a difference, but this is basically a case of what logicians call "making a distinction without a difference." And although habits may result in visible and even undesirable consequences, the assumptions we take for granted without realizing we are doing so can turn friends into foes, and those who should be our allies into enemies.

Without trying to explore this old wisdom here, the point we only want to make is this one. Recognizing what comes across to us as more or less "the same" as what we have previously experienced is necessary for us to be able to make sense of things and events (Verplanken and Orbell 2023: 329; Wood and Rünger 2016: 291).

Awareness—Do facts matter?

Regardless how smart you think you are, or IQ tests have said you must be, it is a lot harder to be intelligent than conventional wisdom says and these tests are supposedly able to predict.

1. **Exposure**—We cannot always be in the right place at the right time to be an eyewitness to things and events. Like it or not, "the facts" we need to know to make wise judgments and good decisions perhaps more often than not must be taken on faith, not firsthand experience. Furthermore, through no fault of our own, all of us can easily be led astray by what others tell us.

2. **Perception**—Even when we are able to witness things and events firsthand, it is no secret that appearances can be deceiving. Furthermore, when we are exposed to something we ought to be taking seriously, we may not be aware of what is happening because we cannot readily perceive what is going on. This is a major reason it is so difficult to decide if we need to be worried about climate change.

3. **Experience**—Despite B. F. Skinner's denial that animals—including our own kind of animal—have minds capable of reaching their own conclusions, it is no secret that the repetition of an experience, as he showed us, can strengthen how predictable what we decide to do may become. The downside of our perfectly normal proclivity to develop habits and assumptions is that both can stifle originality, innovation, and good sense. There is no need to argue that they can lead to inattention and hasty conclusions.

4. **Recognize**—What Daniel Kahneman and others have described as intellectual laziness—our easy willingness to turn to what some call *heuristics* rather than carefully thought-out good sense—can be costly for a reason not always acknowledged. What we intentionally or not commit to memory is usually just the most salient and repetitive features of what we are aware of as sentient creatures. This being so, if something did not come across to us in the past as important, we may not realize or even be able to know whether we have experienced something similar before—as the saying goes, whether we have "been there, done that"—or are dealing with something new, something odd, something unaccountable.

Recognition

As someone who briefly suffered a few years ago from transient global amnesia (TGA) (Ropper 2023), John Terrell knows from his own personal experience that contrary to common sense and conventional wisdom, we do not have to be consciously aware of the world around us to be able to recognize and respond more or less successfully to what we experience in life. The clinical definition of this sudden rupture in a person's ability to deal with reality hints at how unnerving TGA can be. Suddenly you cannot form new memories and may also not be able to recall memories from days, weeks, even years ago. Other people quickly pick up on the fact that something has gone wrong inside your brain because you keep asking the same question over and over again since you cannot remember the answer they have just given you, over and over again.

In John's case, although it evidently seemed to other people that he knew who he was and who they were, he had little awareness of how he was behaving. He simply could not keep track of what was happening in the here and now. He kept asking the same questions. He could not recall things that had happened during the previous year and more. For a day or so, he could neither form new memories, nor recall past events. It was as if he was seeing what he was seeing for the first time.

Researchers have been studying this type of amnesia for more than half a century, yet they are still not sure why it happens (Nehring, Spurling, and Kumar 2023). Fortunately, TGA lasts for only a few hours and at most a day or so. It rarely strikes more than once in a person's lifetime. Other brain functions are not permanently affected. In John's case, the lead neurologist told him the next day that a CT scan done in the middle of the night while he was in the hospital showed not only that all was well up there on his shoulders, but also that "you have the brain of a younger man." The doctor wasn't sure how to respond when John asked him who had been given his old brain.

Setting aside the details of what John went through (and this attempt at humor), this type of personal experience underscores how dependent all of us are on being able to recognize "to connect the dots"—between what we are experiencing in the here and now, and what we have already learned from past experiences (van Ede and Nobre 2023). When something leads to a disconnect between the present and the past, even given the big brain we all have thanks to biology and enough food, we literally cannot make sense of things and events going on around us.

There are many popular and scientific opinions about how the human brain handles—in this age of digital computers, the word often used is *processes*—the incoming streams of sensations it receives from beyond the security of its own bony shell (Graziano 2019: 30–34, 60; Hohwy 2020; Oberauer 2019; Seth 2021). Because we often experience things and events so vividly, so graphically, it is hardly surprising that common sense tells us our memories must be just as rich, detailed, and lively as our conscious thoughts and impressions. Based on what most of us experience in our everyday lives, however, four generalizations seem likely about how we recognize and make sense of things and events.

1. Making sense of what our eyes, ears, and other senses are picking up about what is happening around us (and within us, too) is a dynamic back-and-forth interplay between awareness of things and

events in the here and now, and what we already know about the world from our previous experiences (Xie and Zhang 2022).
2. When it comes to recognizing what our senses are picking up, a little bit goes a long way. Given enough prior experience, we do not need to be hit over the head to sense we may need to pay attention even if we are only seeing something "out of the corner of my eye."
3. For the same reason, it is also easy to jump to conclusions based on surprisingly little evidence.
4. Fortunately, practice makes perfect, or perhaps more realistically—as behaviorists in the last century made a central feature of their influential view of life (see Chapter 2)—repetition can strengthen and improve how well we are able to recognize what may be happening and then respond accordingly, or at least hopefully so (Weisswange et al. 2009).

These elementary observations lead to an obvious question. Call it "prior experience," or call it "memory," how does the human brain know you have experienced something similar before and may already also know how to deal with it? In our ternary model of the mind (Figure 3.2), how is RECOGNITION done?

1. Experience + Hearsay

As Greyson Abid at the University of California, Berkeley, has argued, recognition "straddles the border between perception and cognition," and that it involves a "sensitivity to particulars from one's past" (Abid 2022: 770). As we have already said, however, the particulars in question may not necessarily always be what we have experienced ourselves. They can also be what we have learned about from others, both directly by word-of-mouth, and indirectly through social media, newspapers, books, journal reports, and the like. It is easy to forget that the experiences on which we base so much of dealings with the world do not have to be firsthand—sometimes for better, sometimes for worse.

What may be obvious, nonetheless, is that the act of making sense of things strongly depends on recognizing that you have encountered (or heard about) more or less the same thing before. This is perhaps most vividly documented in the case of people who have been blind from birth, or who have suddenly had their sight restored. Although the evidence about sight restoration following long-term blindness is limited, it seems that it may not be possible to recognize the shapes of things, for example, by sight immediately after regaining your vision (Millar 2019). At least as working propositions, therefore, it seems possible to say:

1. Although no one knows for sure how it is done, the human brain can recognize and try to make sense of the patterning of things and events in space and time at least after repeatedly experiencing (or hearing about) those things and events.
2. We can also learn about the patterning (or purported patterning) of things and events by hearsay from others of our kind. Even then, however, understanding what is being learned depends a lot on what you believe you are hearing, and on how open you are to accepting what you are being told (Mercier and Sperber 2011; Wallace 1961).
3. Although it generally is not a good idea to reduce complex issues down to simple A or B claims, there is some truth in saying recognition can be either *active* (based on firsthand experience) or *passive* (second-hand facts and figures).

2. Memory Tracing

A brain is far too metabolically expensive to have around as a luxury item. In the case of the human brain, for example, it is obvious our offspring take many years to grow up and become functioning adults. It is less obvious, however, that one reason growing up for us takes so long is that our brains make astonishingly high energy demands. It has been documented, for example, that "the brain's metabolic requirements peak in childhood, when it uses glucose at a rate equivalent to 66 percent of the body's resting metabolism and 43 percent of the body's daily energy requirement" (Kuzawa et al. 2014: 13010). The conclusion seems inescapable, although not altogether obvious, that the high cost of human brain development during childhood limits how fast body growth leading to adulthood can also happen.

Even when we are adults, however, having a brain is costly. As an adult, your brain accounts for only about 2 percent of your body weight. It uses, however, about 25 percent of the energy consumed by your body at rest, making it third after skeletal muscle and the liver as the most energy-expensive components of the human body (Fonseca-Azevedo and Herculano-Houzel 2012; Mergenthaler et al. 2013). Given how costly it is to run, "use your brain wisely" is more than just an old expression. As Mark van Rossum (2023) at the University of Nottingham has concluded, "the brain has likely evolved to be able to learn using as little energy as possible."

Given how expensive the human brain is to run, it is not surprising that even with its roughly 86 billion neurons—as we have noted previously—and despite the popular idea that memories, like photographs, vividly capture all that you have experienced in life, our memories (as we have already said) are generally only as detailed and "true to life" as they need to be to see us through from day to day (Eagleman 2011: 27–30, 54; 2015: 56; Seger and Miller 2010). Rather than thinking of our memories as being like photographic images or high-fidelity recordings, our memories are more like artistic impressions than faithful reproductions of the real thing (Graziano 2019). Since memories, however, are commonly believed to be like the latter, we favor calling the memories kept upstairs in our heads *memory traces* (Wood and Rünger 2016).

Figure 3.4 is an attempt to show you what we want the expression "memory trace" to mean. Picture A is a detailed true-to-life raster image of a wolf. Picture B is a simplified version of this same image, emphasizing only what you might need to pay attention to when you encounter a wolf and are deciding whether to "fight or flight" (Chu et al. 2023). However, what is unclear in this imaginative simplification is what sort of an animal is being seen—ambiguity that could lead to making a fatal choice about whether to pat the furry little creature with such a big dark nose, or run for your life. In contrast, Picture C is a minimal trace of Picture A that, unlike Picture B, conveys an essential impression of the beast you are dealing with in a highly streamlined way. To use technical jargon, Picture A is a raster image, and Picture C might be described as a vector image.

3. Parsing

Discovering what exactly are memories and how they form in the brain is one of psychology's enduring research questions (Atkinson and Shiffrin 1968; Baddeley 2012). However, as Freek van Ede at Vrije Universiteit Amsterdam and Anna C. Nobre at the University of Oxford emphasized:

> At any given moment, human behavior is carved out of the external stimulation originating in the environment and of the internal traces in our memories. Contrary to our default understanding of memory as a repository for retrospective recollection, pioneering thinkers in our field have emphasized the fundamental prospective role of memories in guiding our perception and action. The richness of signals in the external environment and countless memories accumulated over various time scales offer boundless possibilities. . . . [S]electing the right information to focus perception and action is a major challenge embedded in our continual interactions with the environment. (van Ede and Nobre 2023: 138)

From this practical perspective, as we said at the beginning of this book, we have found it is helpful to think about the interplay between a brain and the world beyond its protective shell as a give-and-take—a kind of parsing—resulting in memory traces that are patterned in two of the

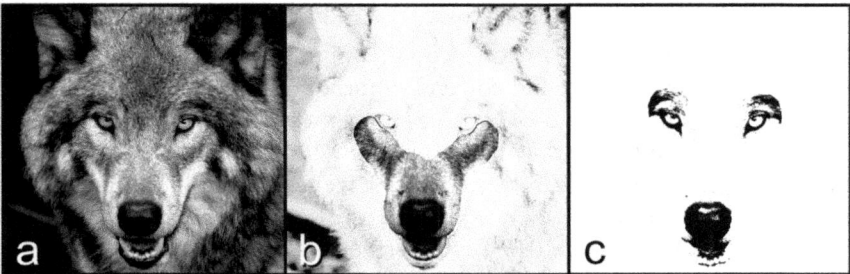

Figure 3.4. What are memories made of? (a) True-to-life raster image of a wolf (this is a 2.36 MB, 300 dpi, jpg image; Source: Steve, Pexel, Public Domain); (b) simplified version of this same image that is unclear about what sort of an animal is being seen—ambiguity that could lead to making a fatal decision (1.89 MB, 300 dpi, jpg image); (c) minimal trace of the same image conveying a critical impression of what you are dealing with in a simplified way (322 KB, 300 dpi, jpg image). © John Edward Terrell

ways in which our experiences are patterned: as *spatial patterns* (Macpherson et al. 2021) and as *temporal patterns* (Zheng et al. 2022). Drawing this distinction is not a denial of the space-time continuum of modern physics. This is just a way of saying that we pay attention to different dimensions of reality when we are forming memory traces because what comes across to us as important is not the abstractions of physics but the realities of life. It is for this reason that we find it useful to talk about two sorts of memory traces—*situational traces* and *sequential traces*—that differ also depending on how strongly they are shaped by change, necessity, or choice (Jacob 1982: 58; Table 3.1).

Table 3.1. Everyday examples of situational and sequential memory traces. © John Edward Terrell

MEMORY TRACE	situational mapping	sequential mapping
CHANCE	finding an available parking space at a grocery store	remembering how to get back to your car in this parking lot
NECESSITY	remembering where your car is located in that parking lot	knowing how to drive to this grocery store
CHOICE	deciding to drive rather than walk to the grocery store	asking how to get to this grocery store

4. Classification

What we have said so far may give you the impression that we think a brain collects memories like a child collects stones of different colors and shapes while walking along a beach, and then stores them away in an old cigar box. As pretty and colorful as they may sometimes be, your memories would be of little use to you if this carefree approach were to prevail. Memories need to be organized to be useful, not just stored away to be admired later from time to time (Aronowitz 2019). Furthermore, although we will not try to resolve the issue, both logic and experience tell us that most of what we are aware of outside our skulls never becomes a memory trace. Instead, much of what is happening around us is sensed but quickly forgotten. Why? Presumably because what we are experiencing from one moment to the next fails to come across to us as memorable even in an impressionistic and rudimentary way. The familiar expressions "been there, done that" and "seen one, seen them all" hint at how remembering things and events evidently involves experiencing them as somehow new and different.

The cognitive psychologist Carol Seger at Colorado State University and her colleague Earl Miller at MIT have remarked: "The ability to group items and events into functional categories is a fundamental characteristic of sophisticated thought" (Seger and Miller 2010: 203). We agree, but we do not see this as characteristic only of sophisticated thought, whatever this qualification should be taken to mean. When dealing with the complex ebb and flow of events and things outside the human skull, how we perceive the world is inherently categorical (Allport 1954: 20). Or as we like to say it, a brain is a pattern recognition device.

Although the word *pattern* can be used in a number of ways, the common thread is that patterns are repeated arrangements of things or events. In contrast, the word *chaos* implies the opposite: a state of disorder that is unintelligible and fundamentally unpredictable. Therefore, seen as a pattern recognition device, any brain worth describing as such tries to remember and later recognize the general (and hopefully more or less predictable) repetitive patterning of things and events going on around it. Chaos, on the other hand, just gives the brain a headache.

Classification is another way to talk about this kind of important mental work. As one website promoting open source software observes:

> Humans are the most amazing pattern-recognition machines. They have the ability to recognize many different types of patterns. If you've ever watched a toddler learn words and concepts, you can almost see the brain neurons firing as the small child starts to recognize patterns for differentiating between objects. Intelligence, then, is really just a matter of being able to store more patterns than anyone else. We could build machines

that could recognize as many chessboard patterns as a chess grandmaster. ("Chaos and Patterns," 2023)

We agree with the authors of this statement that a toddler learning the meaning of words and concepts is a good example of becoming skillful at pattern recognition. Yet saying that how intelligent you are depends on how many patterns you have stored away in your brain is going too far. A game like chess is a highly regimented, rule-based way of generating patterns. The real world is a much more chaotic place.

Consequently, the best our brains can do to help us navigate our way through life (rather than just across a chessboard) is to step back—to generalize—from the particular experiences we have (or others have told us about), and try to find patterns in what we have experienced that are repetitive enough to risk seeing them as good advice and maybe even fairly reliable rules of thumb—what Herbert Simon and Daniel Kahneman (see Chapter 2) have called heuristics (below, Conclusion).

Therefore, although it may not be conventional to do so, we often find ourselves using words like *pattern recognition*, *rules of thumb*, *categorization*, and *classification* perhaps not truly as interchangeable, but nonetheless, as words often coming to mind when we are thinking about how a brain perceives and tries to recognizes things and events outside the confines of the human body. Without this effort at trying to make sense of what is going on around us, the world just looks chaotic and meaningless.

How the brain of any animal including ourselves accomplishes the tack of pattern recognition is mostly a mystery. We have chosen to use the admittedly vague expression "pattern recognition" to sidestep having to resolve the continuing debate in psychology and neuroscience about how conscious, thoughtful, and deliberate people are when they are dealing with the world.

Michael Graziano's attention schema theory (AST), for example, distinguishes between awareness and attention, and credits the brain not only with playing a controlling role in how you move your body and engage with the world physically, but also in what you strategically notice in the world around you (Graziano 2020; Graziano et al. 2019; Graziano and Kasner 2011). "Attention, the deep processing of select items, is one of the most important cognitive operations in the brain. But how does the brain control its attention? One proposed part of the mechanism is that the brain builds a model, or attention schema, that helps monitor and predict the changing state of attention" (Wilterson and Graziano 2021: 1).

You do not have to be an old-fashioned behavioral psychologist like B. F. Skinner to wonder whether the brain builds such a model, or "schema." We prefer, however, to leave it to others to tackle this issue.

The only point we want to make here is that however accomplished, making sense of things and events builds on the brain's ability to find that far from being totally new and unrecognizable, it has experienced similar things and events before and may, therefore, also know what something is, or what may happen next.

The benefits of being able to do this are obvious enough, but the risks involved may not be. Suspecting what may happen next based on your previous experiences in life does not assure that you also know why. As logicians like to say it, one can fall for the fallacy of *post hoc, ergo propter hoc*. A popular example often used on the Internet: "The rooster crows immediately before sunrise; therefore the rooster causes the sun to rise."

Recognition—Making Sense of Things and Events

Making sense of what is happening in the here and now heavily depends on recognizing that you have previously experienced similar situations and events, or have already learned from others about such things.

1. **Experience + hearsay**—We are all dependent on being able to recognize and connect the dots between what we are experiencing in the here and now, and what we have already learned from our past experiences, or have been told about by others. When memory loss leads to a disconnect between the present and the past, we literally cannot make sense of what is happening around us.

2. **Memory tracing**—our memories are generally only as detailed and "true to life" as they need to be to see us through from day to day. They are more like artistic impressions than faithful reproductions of the real thing. For this reason, we favor calling them *memory traces*.

3. **Parsing**—It is helpful to think about the interplay between a brain and the world beyond its protective shell as a give-and-take—a kind of parsing—resulting in memory traces that are patterned in two of the ways in which our experiences are patterned: as *spatial patterns* and as *temporal patterns*.

4. **Classification**—When dealing with the complex ebb and flow of events and things outside the human skull, how we perceive the world is inherently categorical. Or as we like to say it, a brain is a pattern recognition device.

Imagination

The philosopher, historian, and revolutionary Karl Marx (1818–1883) said it well back in the nineteenth century: "A spider conducts operations that resemble those of a weaver, and a bee puts to shame many an architect in the construction of her cells. But what distinguishes the worst architect from the best of bees is this, that the architect raises his structure in imagination before he erects it in reality" (Marx 1887). Something similar can be said about the role of imagination in daily life. What are popularly called our "powers of imagination" are not only the keys to understanding what is happening in the here and now. Imagination is also needed to decide how we may be able to control what we expect—and sometimes fear—may happen next.

Much of what has been written about the psychology of imagination was recently summarized in *The Cambridge Handbook of the Imagination*, edited by Anna Abraham (2020). The 68 authors in the 48 chapters in this collection cover most aspects of the topic, with a special focus on brain function—neuroanatomy and neurophysiology. Of more concern for the present book are the connections these authors find between imagination and intelligence.

One of these authors, Bernard Crespi, takes a forthright stand: "As defined here, imagination and intelligence are essentially opposite to one another, with imagination involving generation of the unreal, and intelligence involving analysis and comprehension of the real" (Crespi 2020: 773). At the other end of a spectrum of opinion is Rex Jung, who tells us how he moved beyond seeing intelligence as simply *"rapid and accurate problem-solving"* (Jung 2020: 549; his italics).

Jung was inspired by studies of the behavior of crows to ask himself where he could find their "cognitive flexibility, imagination, and prospection" in human behavior. It was not lost on him that even the original measure of intelligence, invented by Alfred Binet, included measures of creativity. "Intelligence and creativity have been entangled with one another from the very beginning. So, from the world of 'rapid and accurate' problem-solving, I ventured into the world of 'novel and useful' problem-solving." (2020: 549). This ultimately led him to conclude: "if there is one cognitive construct that might separate human progress from that of other higher mammals it very likely involves the singular capacity of imagination" (2020: 558).

1. Memory Traces

What is often labeled as imagination generally includes all of the expectations we have about what may happen next that are more complex than just assuming the sun will rise tomorrow and the weather will probably be clear; that is, if it doesn't rain. Even anticipating what to eat tomorrow, for lunch perhaps, involves imagining, although surely simple-minded animals can manage this much forecasting.

More notable is the realization that even our memory traces are a kind of imagination. As we said earlier, they are merely our impressions of things and events going on outside our heads. Sometimes they may just "come to mind" seemingly unprovoked. But when we want to recall them intentionally, we usually have to imagine what was happening in the past and what we were dealing with back then.

2. Recall

Like the rest of us, Gene Anderson can vividly remember scenes from his childhood, but not the humdrum details leading up to them. Like all the rest of us, he needs to fill in the details of those scenes from the past using his imagination. After all, he has not "been there" for decades. This does not mean our memories of the past and our expectations based on them about what may happen in the future are false. Quite the contrary. What is popularly called "using your imagination" is as necessary for the retrieval of factual knowledge as it is to what is commonly called simply *imagining* (creating unreal and wholly counterfactual scenes and situations).

Good examples of the practical importance of fantasy and imagination in our lives would be myths and folktales. Everywhere on earth, these products of the human mind encode social morals, serve as guides to life, and help organize how we see the world. They are part of what is generally called religion (Durkheim 1995 [1912]). They can also be simple everyday teaching stories that mix reality and fantasy inextricably. The perfectly ordinary child next door, for example, goes out into a world that slowly becomes strange, and she or he eventually confronts a giant, a monster, or a guiding spirit—which teaches them a moral in a direct and forceful way (see e.g., Anderson and Pierotti [2022] for an extended analysis of such stories).

3. Recombination

The creative interplay between memory and imagination within the human brain is not just a psychological issue. Novels for instance, effectively celebrate this intellectual partnership, this combination of seeming fact and actual fiction, especially novels of the common type known in French as a *roman à clef*, a "novel with a key." This form of storytelling is based heavily on fact, but the result is not an historical novel intended to be a true-to-case. A roman à clef has characters drawn from life who are doing some things that their real-life originals did, but also quite a few wholly imaginary things. Perhaps the greatest is the eighteenth-century Chinese novel *The Story of the Stone* (Cao 1973–1986) showing that blending fact and fiction in storytelling in ways that cannot be easily teased out or analyzed is not something unique to the English-speaking world.

Much of our lives are lived more or less in this fashion. We mix reality with dreams, hopes, wishes, and projections in ways that lead us to play roles in real life as if we were someone in true-to-life novels. Seen this way, intelligence involves the weaving together of perception and innovative thinking in what are complex and often far from predictable patterns. The mind makes structures, from simple opposition (Lévi-Strauss 1962) to extremely elaborate cognitive maps (Arzy and Dafni-Merom 2020; Lynch 1960) and even more elaborate processes, systems, and dynamic structures (Sternberg 2015: 103–5).

There is really no need to add that dreams, too, are another way that our brains are able to create imaginary worlds where fantasy and memory are recombined and mixed in ways that sometimes seem predictable (given, say, our recent experiences while awake), and yet sometimes are wildly improbable and unrealistic. In many places on earth, people also intentionally engage in activities involving meditation, trance, and other dreamlike practices that lead to visionary experiences validating their religious and spiritual beliefs (see e.g., Collerton, Perry, and Robert 2020; also Anderson and Pierotti 2022; Humphrey and Onon 1996.

4. New Memory Traces

Architects, painters, composers, and indeed anyone getting off a good line of poetry or thinking up a new tune all draw on the human capacity to innovate. Songbirds, too, can innovate much of their auditory repertoire. Some, such as mockingbirds and thrashers, are extremely brilliant and original when they do so. Yet their innovations are confined to a tiny realm of expression—song—and perhaps also to a little creative nest-building. To offer another example, wolves are able to think up new hunting patterns and tricks that they can communicate to those they are running with on a chase. Yet their inventiveness, too, does not go much beyond this.

These several examples show that having an imagination is not solely a human characteristic. Perhaps what is most human about our own species' capacity to recombine the memories we have gained from experiences (and hearsay) and shape them into new ideas, new memory traces, is that our flights of fantasy can become so real to us that we lose sight of their origin inside our heads. We may come to mistake them for what is

> ## Imagination—Our Strength and Weakness as a Species
>
> What are popularly called our "powers of imagination" are the keys to understanding what is happening in the here and now. They enable us to anticipate and plan for—and sometimes fear—what may happen next. Unfortunately, what we imagine to be true can also be our downfall.
>
> 1. **Memory traces**—Our memories are our impressions of things and events going on outside our heads. Although at times old memories may come to mind seemingly unprovoked, we often need to imagine what may have happened in the past to be able to recall what actually did happen—as well as we are able to do so.
>
> 2. **Recall**—Myths and folktales are two of the ways we use our powers of imagination to remember how we are supposed to deal with life, its social demands, and frequent challenges.
>
> 3. **Recombination**—The creative interplay between memory and imagination within the human brain can lead both to useful inspiration and dangerous delusions.
>
> 4. **New memory traces**—Our ability as human beings to mix and recombine our memories can lead to new ideas, new memory traces, that seem so real to us we risk losing sight of their origin inside our heads. We may come to mistake these new memory traces for what is true and factual about the world outside our skulls. When this happens, our creative advantages over other species may not only lead us astray; they may also prove to be dangerous and destructive.

true about the world outside our skulls. Then our creative advantages over other species may not just lead us astray. They can also be destructive.

In recent years there have been public warnings about the dangers and potentially unmanageable risks to society and global security of AI (artificial intelligence) computer systems. The mathematical neural networks being developed in AI can enable computers to learn from their mistakes and make intelligent decisions without direct human assistance (Macpherson et al. 2021). The downside, however, is that they can also generate wildly inaccurate and even offensively false claims and assertions. As one

AI expert has remarked: "We now have systems that can interact with us through natural language, and we can't distinguish the real from the fake" (Metz 2023).

It may be comforting to believe that since we are human beings and not machines, we are less likely to mistake what we imagine to be true for what is really so. However, as we said at the beginning of this book, what do all of us need to do to make this claim more than merely a self-serving delusion?

Redefining Intelligence

According to Paul De Boeck and his colleagues at Ohio State University and the Pontifical Catholic University of Chile, intelligence is both the most successful idea in psychology when it comes to measurement, and yet is also famous for being impossible to define (De Boeck et al. 2020: 70). They tell us, however, not to worry about intelligence being "a concept without an essence." Why not? Because, they say, intelligence exists in the same sense as most of our everyday concepts such as "sadness," "joy," "love," "altruism," etc. that have meanings, too, despite being only "rather loose somewhat overlapping clusters of exemplars." In defense of this claim, they point to the Italian dish called *saltimbocca* (page 4). It has no fixed culinary definition, and yet it can be found on restaurant menus around the world. Similarly, the word *intelligence* "can be found on the menu of research in psychology" despite not being "a clear concept, and, based on the lack of consensus regarding its definition, it is possible that it never will be."

Why do De Boeck and his colleagues not see this as a problem? Because, they say, experts "agree on many examples of intelligence and on many counterexamples, even without a definition, and there also is a gray zone where experts have contradictory opinions." Therefore, "the lack of a definition of intelligence does not prevent its measurement from being useful and having predictive value, just as one who orders saltimbocca has some idea of what to expect."

In 1964, U.S. Supreme Court Justice Potter Stewart used the colloquial expression "I know it when I see it" to explain why a film claimed to be pornographic by the State of Ohio was not obscene, and was therefore, constitutionally protected (Gewirtz 1996). It would seem that De Boeck and his colleagues may want us to accept the same rationale to decide what is and what isn't intelligence.

We do not accept the claim by B. F. Skinner (see Chapter 2) and other behavioral psychologists that there is nothing to write about (Table 3.2).

But we also do not accept that because intelligence is an idea that defies definition, it makes no difference where you start off in the quest for understanding. Maybe you will still end up with something to write about. But why would anyone bother? One of our favorite saying is "If you start off on the wrong foot, you will still end up somewhere."

In the parable of the blind men and the elephant there really is, as the saying goes, an elephant in the room. In this chapter, we have adopted a different tactic, a different strategy, from that usually used to write about how the human brain engages with the world. We have asked how this metaphorical elephant, so to speak, behaves—what does it need to be able to do—even though we cannot look inside this beast to see how its body works and why it behaves the way it does rather than in some other fashion.

Instead of agreeing with de Boeck and his colleagues that intelligence adds up to "rather loose somewhat overlapping clusters of exemplars," in this chapter we have now described three fundamental abilities, three basic mental talents, we see as instrumental in helping all of us do what we need and want to do in life: awareness, recognition, and imagination. We are not, however, the first to propose that intelligence, whatever you take this word to mean, can be broken down into a number of parts, components, or ingredients.

In 1983, for example, the research psychologist Howard Gardner at Harvard University challenged the idea that there is just one type of "all-purpose" intelligence, general intelligence (sometimes called "little g"), that can be measured effectively by intelligence tests. As others had before and since, he has argued that the purpose of intelligence is achieving success at problem-solving, but unlike those who equate intelligence with "g," he argues that to be successful, different human careers and accomplishments require different sorts of intelligence: linguistic, logical-mathematical, spatial, musical, bodily-kinesthetic, interpersonal, and so on (Kornhaber 2020: 662). In other words, one shoe does not fit all.

Also in the 1980s, Robert Sternberg, then at Yale and now at Cornell University, was promoting what he was calling his "triarchic model of intelligence." Like others before and since, he accepted the view that intelligence can be defined as "purposive adaptation to, shaping of, and selection of real-world environments relevant to one's life" (Sternberg 1984: 271). As he has recently explained:

> Successful intelligence is (1) the ability to formulate, strive for, and, to the extent possible, achieve one's goals in life, given one's sociocultural context, (2) by capitalizing on strengths and correcting or compensating for weaknesses (3) in order to adapt to, shape, and select environments

Table 3.2. Defining ingredients of intelligence as seen from differing perspectives on what it means to be human. © John Edward Terrell

FUNDAMENTALS	chance	necessity	choice
behavioral psychology	stimulus	response	— — —
conventional definitions	skill	cleverness	control
basic mental abilities	awareness	recognition	imagination

(4) through a combination of analytical, creative, and practical abilities. In recent years, I have emphasized that intelligence best serves individuals and societies when it is augmented by wisdom. (Sternberg 2020a: 680)

Appropriately, Sternberg calls this way of thinking about how our minds work "successful intelligence." He emphasizes that "there may be no one set of behaviors that is 'intelligent' for everyone, because people can adjust to their environments in different ways" (1984: 272).

Even if there is little agreement nowadays on how to define intelligence, and different ways, nonetheless, to write about what this word can mean, there still often is a common set of underlying assumptions about how skillful, clever, and controlling you need to be to accomplish what you want or need to do in life (Table 3.2). Such a performance-based understanding of this word also commonly assumes that the goal of taking note of intelligence, whatever this is taken to mean, is basically to be able to evaluate—and judge—how well each of us is able to do something seen as somehow important and worth doing. Yet this interpretation of what this word refers to is open-ended enough to apply not just to intellectuals of one description or another, but to football players, trapeze acrobats, and even scam artists.

If this is all this familiar word means, why not just say being intelligent means "being good at what you do . . . whatever it is you are doing"?

Levels of Awareness

The idea that intelligence can be divided—somewhat like Caesar's famous claim about a part of ancient Europe called Gaul—into three divisions, skills, or talents is an old one in psychology (Tigner and Tigner 2000). We

Table 3.3. Intelligence reinterpreted as levels of awareness. © John Edward Terrell.

INTELLIGENCE LEVEL	chance	necessity	choice
mechanical awareness	experience	recognition	imagination
functional awareness	observe	assume	decide
relational awareness	survey	theory	model
intuitive perception	fantasy	belief	delusion

do not think there are three *kinds* of intelligence, but rather three *levels of awareness* at which we use our brains to do what they are capable of doing (Table 3.3).

1. Mechanical Awareness

Human beings are not about to grow wings and fly. Both biology and the real world clearly set limits on what we can do as individuals and as a species. Within those limits, however, we are a remarkably inventive species, although we are not always well and adequately informed. (The example of climate change speaks for itself, or rather we wish it could.)

Given these basic facts of life, debating nature vs. nurture seems pointless. As V. S. Ramachandran has argued, believing an IQ test can measure something biologically inherited called general intelligence, or "little g," is like thinking general health is a singular thing because how long you live "has a strong heritable component that can be expressed as a single number—age!" And yet, as he goes on to say, whole careers in psychology and politics "have been built on the equally absurd belief in single measurable general intelligence" (Ramachandran 2011: 171). Or as psychologist Ken Richardson said just as bluntly, genetic studies may aim to untangle the complex interplay between genes and environments. But attempting this completely misses the point. Understanding the nature of the tangle, not the untangled, should be the goal of research. "It is precisely in such tangles that heritabilities go missing and intelligent life is born—and a 'grown-up' science might become possible" (Richardson 2012: 595).

What we call *mechanical awareness* is merely our way to acknowledge that instead of trying to pin down which part of the brain does what sort of work, in this chapter, all we have attempted is to determine three types of work the brain needs to do at this fundamental down-to-earth level of engagement with the real world: awareness, recognition, and imagination.

2. Functional Awareness

When we are actively—and more or less consciously—engaged with the world outside our skulls, rather than calling what we are doing merely being aware of what is going on, we consider that a better word to use acknowledging the directness of what is being done is the verb *observe* (Table 3.3). Furthermore, recognizing things and events demands more than simply identifying whether or not what is out there in the world is "the same" or at least "very similar" to what we have previously experienced. Hence, rather than using the word *recognition* when talking about how the mind makes sense of things and events—and also as a way to acknowledge it is always possible to be wrong in how we are dealing with things and events—is to use the verb *assume*.

Finally, when what is involved is not just our thoughtfulness as human beings, but also our actions, what is meant by the word *imagination* seems too open-ended. Does this word refer not only to our remembered recollections of previous things and events, but also to our developing *concepts*, *fantasies*, and *intentions*? What does it mean to say "use your imagination"? Without claiming a single word can resolve such questions, we think a better word to use is the verb *decide* not only in the conventional sense of "to choose something, especially after thinking carefully about several possibilities," but also in the sense of wanting to achieve some change or outcome.

Although in this chapter we have not described what we see as the basic cognitive steps of functional awareness (Figure 3.5) in the detailed way we have tried to write about some of the primary elements of mechanical awareness, we want to point out how different our understanding of what is involved is from what was acceptable to B. F. Skinner and other behavioral psychologists during much of the twentieth century.

3. Relational Awareness

We have repeatedly described the brain in this book as a pattern recognition device. We stand by this description, but what is meant by making sense of things and events—and seeing what can be done to control things and events down the road of time—often also means playing an active role not only in what is happening, but what will happen as time goes by. We have also suggested that memory traces can be thought of as two differing sorts of pattern recognition: *situational* and *sequential* memory traces.

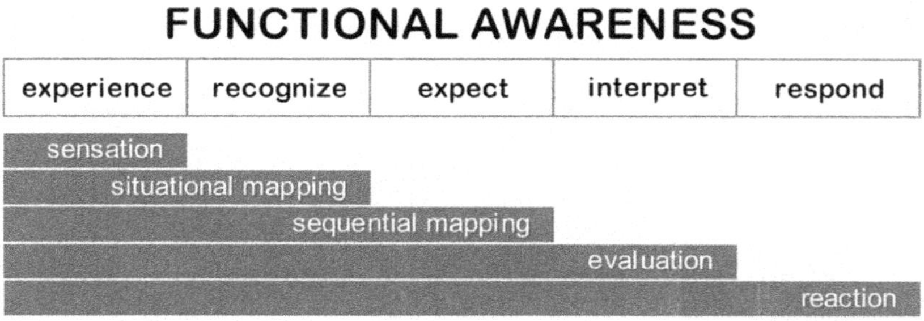

FUNCTIONAL AWARENESS

experience	recognize	expect	interpret	respond

- sensation
- situational mapping
- sequential mapping
- evaluation
- reaction

Figure 3.5. Although some psychologists during the twentieth century were willing to analyze the behavior of animals, including human beings, as the pairing of a stimulus with a particular response, even then it was widely recognized that individuals play critical roles in what happens to them (Woodworth and Schlosberg 1954). Adopting our terminology, functional awareness can be thought of as going down five steps, or stages, of engagement with the world beyond the confines of the skull. © John Edward Terrell.

From this general perspective, what we mean by relational awareness can be described in a number of ways, but the basic idea is that keeping track of how the patterning of things and events changes over time and space is what needs to be done to try to understand why things exist and events happen . . . and what can be done to change the order and results of such things and events.

4. Intuitive Perception

Dictionaries say *intuitive* means being "able to know or understand something because of feelings rather than facts or proof." Giving all the credit for figuring things out, however, to something called "feelings" ignores what would otherwise be obvious. Call it "laziness" as Kahneman has, or "heuristics" as he, Gigerenzer, and others would, given sufficient experience with the world and its ways, most of us find it is possible to get by from day to day with surprisingly little active awareness of what we are doing. Ironically, our feelings may have little to do with what we feel we know and understand.

The challenge of relational awareness is that paying attention to what is happening around us means staying aware of what is going on, and not relying solely and simply on our memories, our impressions, our intuitions gained from what we have experienced previously. As we discuss in the next and concluding chapter, this is harder to do than it may sound. One of the main reasons is that while our intuitive perceptions of things and events may often work in our favor, they also let us get away with paying less attention to "facts or proof" than may be good for us. Hearsay and the verbally expressed wisdom of others, however honest and well-meaning, can be helpful and sometimes even essential. Like it or not, however, there is no real alternative to being directly in touch with what is happening around us. Some would call this "science." But it can also be called just old-fashioned good sense.

Key Points

1. Instead of seeing intelligence as something we all have to a greater or lesser degree, it is more useful to say that what it means to be intelligent is the interplay, or balance, among three basic cognitive skills or talents: awareness, recognition, and imagination.
2. Since we must rely so heavily in life on hearsay rather than on our own experiences, other animals—since they cannot rely as strongly as we do on verbal communication—could be described as more intelligent than we are.
3. Seen as a pattern recognition device, the brain works to remember and later recognize the general (and more or less expectable) repetitive patterning of things and events going on around it.
4. Our powers of imagination are not just the keys to understanding what is happening in the here and now. They are also needed to deal with what may happen down the road.

Conclusion

Being Intelligent

It has long been accepted that how intelligent we are is mostly a matter of nature (biology and genetics) and not nurture (what we have learned since we were born). We have argued instead that this word means both how and how well we are able to connect with the world and others around us on three levels of engagement beyond the confines of our skulls: *mechanical awareness*, *functional awareness*, and *relational awareness*.

In *The Economist* in November 1955, C. Northcote Parkinson, who was teaching then at the University of Malaya in Singapore as Raffles Professor of History, offered the world a humorous commentary pompously titled "Parkinson's Law." With feigned seriousness, statistical data, and even mathematical equations, he compared the efficiency (or rather the lack thereof) of civil service bureaucracies with this now well-known (although nowadays rather biased) example:

> It is a commonplace observation that work expands so as to fill the time available for its completion. Thus, an elderly lady of leisure can spend the entire day in writing and despatching a postcard to her niece at Bognor Regis. An hour will be spent in finding the postcard, another in hunting for spectacles, half-an-hour in a search for the address, an hour and a quarter in composition, and twenty minutes in deciding whether or not to take an umbrella when going to the pillar-box in the next street. The total effort which would occupy a busy man for three minutes all told may in this fashion leave another person prostrate after a day of doubt, anxiety and toil. (Parkinson 1955: 635)

The editors of *The Economist* saw fit to introduce this groundbreaking explanation decades ago with a similarly playful editorial preamble: "The report of the Royal Commission on the Civil Service was published on

Thursday afternoon. Time has not permitted any comment in this week's issue of *The Economist* on the contents of the Report. But the startling discovery enunciated by a correspondent in the following article is certainly relevant to what should have been in it."

We take no position on the credibility of Parkinson's Law, although it strikes us as a worthy attempt to understand the otherwise inscrutable growth of bureaucracies not just in civil service but in academic settings, as well. We introduce his law here to illustrate perhaps one of the most glaring weaknesses of seeing intelligence, whatever this is, as something that is solely focused on the sober and demanding realities of the often-touted struggle for existence. Being really good at computer games, playing soccer, and winning at chess may or may not have something to do with one's allegedly measurable IQ. Any theory of intelligence, however, that neglects to include play, reading for pleasure, and the performance arts is surely missing too much about what it means to be human (Flynn 1997; Flynn 2007). Or for that matter, a dog. And taking more time than perhaps necessary to do something is not a sign of stupidity.

Saying only this, however, overlooks what may be Parkinson's real point. Much of what we do in life—many of the goals we have for ourselves, or are assigned to us by others—are arbitrary rather than necessary. How quickly and well we achieve them—or to use words Herbert Simon favored, how "optimally rational" are the ways we use (Chapter 2)—may make little real or practical difference. More to the point, although just as easily overlooked, there is often more than one way to succeed. Travel around the globe, for instance, and try to keep track of all the different ways to say "thank you." Or how to use your credit card. Not to mention how many different ways there are to cook a meal and call it *saltimbocca* (page 2).

The Obvious is Seldom Seen

In his now famous commentary, Parkinson uses his sense of humor to say something serious. We cannot match his wit, but in this book we have something to offer we see as similarly worth saying. When intelligence is primarily seen as problem solving, and solving problems well is said to be critically important, not only is problem solving well often taken as a sign of high intelligence, but also a sign of being able to do important things, perhaps quite remarkable things. We think, however, that there is more to life than solving problems in speedy and efficient ways.

Twice before in this book we have mentioned what a high school Physics teacher so often liked to say years ago that this observation became something of a joke among his students: "The obvious is seldom seen." He never told us how he knew this. We don't think he had in mind what is called the Troxler Effect. Even so, this effect illustrates an obvious truth. Before you can solve a problem however well or poorly, however fast or slowly, you must first see whatever it is as a problem.

This famous illusion was discovered in 1804 by the Swiss physician Ignaz Troxler (1780–1866). He found that if you stare at something intently, what surrounds what you are staring at seems to fade and disappear slowly from view (Eagleman 2020: 161–63). This happens because your eyes have been designed by evolution to pick up what is changing in your visual field, not what remains the same. So although you are not aware of it, your eyeballs are constantly jiggling (due to tiny involuntary movements called *saccades*) that help keep your eyes "wide open," so to speak, by keeping the cells of your retina receptive to further visual stimulation (Alexander et al. 2018; Poletti and Rucci 2016).

We invoke this optical illusion to illustrate that once you have gained an impression (a memory trace) of a thing or event by experiencing it, it may take more than just the blink of an eye or the jiggle of your head to get you to pay attention again to something similar happening around you. And more to the point, perhaps then change the impression you have already gained of what is going on and why.

As ironic as it may sound, therefore, experience is both the best teacher and also the worst enemy your brain can have. Although someone like Daniel Kahneman (see Chapter 2) might accuse you of being lazy for not being careful and paying adequate attention, we think it is only fair to acknowledge that not paying attention to things and events is not simply a sign of inherent foolishness, carelessness, or stupidity. We all are only human. Like it or not, wise or not, sometimes we do not do something we ought to do simply because we see no reason to do it.

The ABCs of Intelligence

Some have argued that social scientists are often naive enough to believe *nurture* (learning and the environment) always wins out over *nature* (biology and genetics) in determining what we all do, say, and think (Pinker 2002). If you have read this far in this book, you know we think this claim is rhetorical rather than truthful (pages 33–34). We introduced the convention of the ternary plot in Chapter 1 to make it visually obvious that debates about A or B are misleading at best, and basically foolish. Nobody we know would claim that biology and genetics have nothing to do with what it means to be human.

In this book, we have found it useful instead to talk about three basic mental abilities or talents—awareness, recognition, and imagination. There is nothing magical, however, about saying there are three ways to think about how we all handle things and events going on around us. Moreover, as we remarked at the end of the last chapter and not the three we have in mind, Robert Sternberg was becoming famous decades ago for also saying that intelligence can be seen in three different ways (Sternberg 1984). And let's not forget Freud, too, not only subdivided the human psyche into his three famous characters—the id, ego, and superego—but also subdivided our awareness of the world into three levels—the conscious, preconscious, and unconscious mind—although these are not those we have talked about in this book (Morin 2006).

Therefore, although there is nothing special about the number 3, in Chapter 1 we started using ternary plots as a way of making it obvious (we hope) that what happens in life is rarely (maybe never) a matter of just one thing or another. Life is complex and causation is similarly so. It is both wise and helpful to think about things and events as the balance of numerous contingencies, not just A or B, A and B, or even A, B, and C.

Yet one must start somewhere. We have opted in this book to sketch for you our observations, ideas, and propositions three at a time.

Basic Intelligence

The evolutionary history of life on Earth shows there are and have long been many ways to survive and make a living. At the same time, it is also clear that there are certain basic biologically facilitated skills and abilities that are vitally needed regardless of how you implement and use them. Although we have not tried to speculate about what might be the physical underpinnings of what we have called mechanical awareness (see Chapter 3), there is evidence showing how this basic set of skills is supported by the biological realities of being human.

1. Awareness and Alzheimer's Disease

Alzheimer's disease is a form of dementia that gradually destroys a person's cognitive skills—awareness, recognition, and imagination—that can ultimately lead to an inability to carry out even simple tasks. Alzheimer's usually first shows up later in life, mostly after the age of 65 years or so. In the United States, it is the seventh leading cause of death. Why this degenerative decline occurs is still not well understood. Nobody knows why it usually affects older adults. According to the U.S. National Institute on Aging, age-related changes include shrinking of parts of the brain, inflammation, blood vessel damage, and other detectable signs of deterioration ("Alzheimer's Disease" 2023). Classic symptoms include memory loss, wandering, getting lost, trouble handling money and paying bills, repeatedly asking the same questions, and other changes in behavior that may ultimately lead to the inability to speak and total dependence on others for life's necessities.

2. Recognition and Post-Traumatic Stress Disorder (PTSD)

According to the U.S. National Institute of Mental Health, anyone can develop Post-Traumatic Stress Disorder (PTSD) at any age, not only combat veterans but anyone who has experienced, witnessed, or even simply heard about a physical or sexual assault, abuse, an accident, a disaster, a terror attack, or other sort of terrifying event ("PTSD" 2023). People afflicted may feel stressed or frightened, even when they are not in danger. Reportedly about seven or eight people out of a hundred will experience PTSD at some time in their life. Women are more likely to develop PTSD than men. Symptoms—including flashbacks reliving the traumatic event along with physical symptoms such as a racing heart or sweating—usually begin within three months of a traumatic incident, but they may show up even years later. Not only can thoughts and feelings trigger these symptoms, but also words, objects, or situations that are reminders of what happened. Symptoms must last longer than one month for the disability to be classified medically as PTSD. They must be severe enough to interfere with normal life, such as relationships and work. Those suffering from PTSD commonly also deal with depression, substance use, or one or more anxiety disorders. Some people recover within half a year; for others, symptoms may last for a year or longer.

3. Imagination and Autism Spectrum Disorder (ASD)

According to the U.S. National Institute of Mental Health, autism spectrum disorder (ASD) is a neurological and developmental disorder affecting how people behave, interact with others, communicate, and learn ("Autism" 2023). Autism is called a developmental disorder because symptoms usually appear in the first two years of life. People with ASD commonly have difficulty communicating and interacting with other people, have restricted interests and repetitive behaviors, and other symptoms affecting their ability to function well in school, work, and other areas of life. They are likely to have difficulty handling social situations, making friends, and sharing imaginative play. However, autism is called a spectrum disorder because there is wide variation in the type and severity of the symptoms experienced. What causes this disorder is almost completely unknown, although there is evidently an increased likelihood of developing ASD if you have a sibling with ASD, older parents, Down syndrome, or very low birth weight.

Given these three examples—Alzheimer's Disease, PTSD, and autism—it is obvious that biology plays a critical role in mechanical awareness. Nobody we know would argue that what you *can* do and sometimes maybe even *will* do does not depend on having the means to do so. The only useful argument would be how likely it is that any of us will do something merely because it happens to be something we can do. After all, we can't walk the way we do without legs, but where we go doesn't depend on having two legs to stand on (or four, if you are a dog, a horse, or some other quadruped).

As the old saying goes, "doing what comes naturally" definitely needs to be one of the reasons why we do what we do as human beings (Figure 1.2b).

Functional and Relational Awareness

What about the other two levels of awareness (Figure 4.1) in our model of what it means to be intelligent? Using the causal triangle we introduced in Chapter 1 as our guide, what we have just said about *mechanical awareness* is about WHAT we are able to be aware of that is happening outside our skulls. From this perspective, what we call *functional awareness* is about HOW we all then deal with things and events "out there." Awareness at this level involves active, immediate, and subjective engagement with what is happening, and is sometimes but not always both conscious and intentional.

It is the third level of engagement with things and events, *relational awareness*, that is both most distinctively (but not uniquely) human, and also the most problematic. We all are the only species, for example, that can come up with a claim such as "I think she was right in what she said." Why? Because other animals apparently cannot handle dependent clauses. We are not, however, the only creatures who can look for—*survey*—connections between actions and reactions, means and ends. Even so, when we want to understand WHY things exist, and why things happen, we are the ones who are skilled at coming up with plausible explanations—*theories*—and it is our species that is the skilled one at defending why the ideas and claims we come up with should be taken seriously as *models* of reality. The world's many religions are telling examples of how insistent we can be in defending our insights about—our models of—reality.

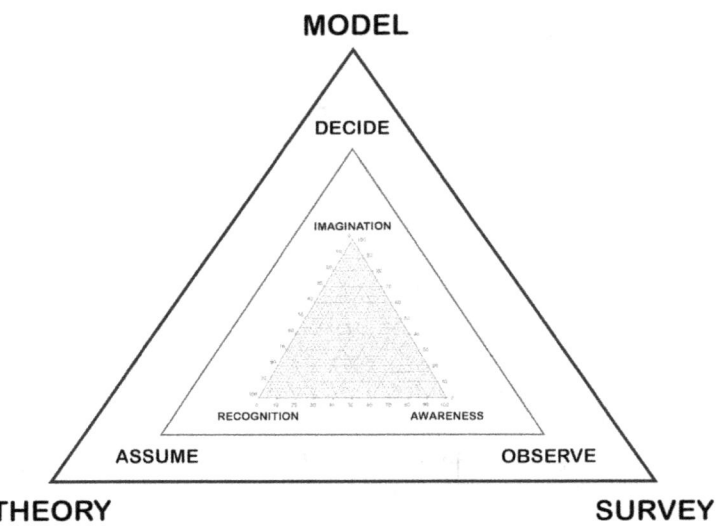

Figure 4.1. In this book, we suggest that acting intelligently can be thought of as a dynamic interplay of mental skills on three different levels of engagement with the opportunities we have and challenges we face in life. © John Edward Terrell.

Mythical Intelligence and Practical Realities

The American folklorist Alan Dundes years ago remarked that some folklorists object strongly when other academics or someone with a political ax to grind take the word *myth* too freely to mean *error* or *fallacy*. Properly understood, such folklore purists insist, myths are not to be seen as true or false, right or wrong. Rather, myths are sacred oral narratives explaining how the earth and its inhabitants came to be as they now are (Dundes 1971).

As Dundes acknowledged, what you call something—how you classify it as a *this* or a *that*, as good or bad, and so forth—can be helpful when you need to find it again, or at least something like it. It is not misleading, for example, to say that what we have been calling *memories* and *memory traces* are practical ways our bodies and our brains make sense of what we are experiencing. But here is the problem. As Dundes asked, how universal is any classification likely to be?

> Is what American folklorists consider under the genre label "proverb" the same as what a German folklorist calls a *Sprichwort* or what a Japanese folklorist calls *kotowaza*? We are aware of the fact that in any one

culture there may be a difference between folk or native categories on the one hand and analytic categories on the other. What the folk in the United States might term "old sayings," the American folklorist might group under "superstition," "proverb," etc. But what are the criteria for the establishment of these various analytic categories? And to what extent are these criteria applicable to folkloristic materials from other cultures? (1971: 94)

As an example, he offers this observation along with others: "How would American folklorists classify the idea that when it thunders, God is moving his furniture, or that potato carts are rolling across the sky, or that two clouds are bumping their heads together, or that angels are rolling stones downhill?" (1971: 94–95).

As a way around the issue of what should or shouldn't be called folklore, Dundes suggested we use the label *folk idea*:

By "folk ideas," I mean traditional notions that a group of people have about the nature of man, of the world, and of man's life in the world. Folk ideas would not constitute a genre of folklore but rather would be expressed in a great variety of different genres. Proverbs would almost certainly represent the expression of one or more folk ideas, but the same folk ideas might also appear in folktales, folksongs, and in fact almost every conventional genre of folklore, not to mention nonfolkloristic materials. (1971: 95)

Call it a folk idea, a basic premise, or whatever words you favor. If intelligence is taken to be somehow "about the nature of man, of the world, and of man's life in the world" (apologizing for the quoted use of the word "man"), then it seems easier to understand why this word is still popular even though nobody has defined it in a way that works at least for most of us.

Whether this is a good thing is debatable. The children's rhyme "sticks and stones may break my bones, but words will never harm me" dates back in one form or another at least to the early nineteenth century. This sentiment is a positive one. There is no doubt, however, that the word intelligence can be used to harm as well as help us.

Calibrating Human Worth

It is an easily observable fact that we are a diverse species in many ways. We also don't all do everything equally well. Or as quickly as others do. Is it surprising, therefore, that it is widely accepted that there must be something lodged inside us—something that can be labeled as intelligence—making us different from one another? And different not just in trivial ways, but sometimes in ways that are locally valued as important, wise, and wonderful? Is it also a mystery why some would want us to keep this old word in our dictionaries? And why some are prepared to use it to bolster their own sense of self-worth and claim to be better than other people?

As discussed in Chapter 1, Lewis Terman at Stanford University was renowned for his professional interest in the study of intelligence. He also believed in eugenics. He was committed to the idea that the human race can be improved by selective breeding in the way that desirable varieties of dogs, cows, and racehorses can be created by choosing who gets to live and who must die before they are able to mate with others of their kind. Terman did not invent IQ testing. He did help develop and promote, however, this purportedly objective way of rating the value of a human life.

The rest, as the saying goes, is history. He and others used this way to evaluate the basic worth of Indigenous, Mexican, and Black communities and immigrants—and, yes, also those with limited mental abilities whom he labeled as "feeble-minded" (those with an IQ of under 70; Terman 1917), those committed to non-conforming gender roles, homosexuals, and the like—vis-à-vis what they saw as the inherently refined biological traits of White Americans.

The durability of intelligence as a folk idea, therefore, derives at least in part from the reality that this view of what it means to be human can be used to judge others in a seemingly impartial and objective way. Both history and current events today show that keeping this word in our working vocabulary, therefore, may come at a cost that is not worth paying. It is also clear that not everyone sees what people in Europe and the United States talk about as intelligence the way people there do.

Global Perspectives

The belief that everybody around the world would answer the question "What is intelligence?" more or less the same way rests on the faulty assumption that everywhere on Earth people are trying to do more or less the same things for the same reasons. In a short book like this one, we can only offer you two more examples showing that this elementary assumption is far from the truth.

The cost of the folk idea of "intelligence" for people of Te Moana-nui-a-kiwa *(Pacific Ocean)*

The concept of intelligence as a marker of ability and "progress" has historically cost Pacific peoples dearly. This Western folk idea is entwined for Indigenous Pacific people in a history of suppression and colonial categorization. The effect has been substantial, and can still be seen today in how people are judged using this foreign idea as the only valid way to evaluate their worthiness and potential success.

Pacific people have been analyzed and categorized in this fashion for hundreds of years, as seen through such examples as Durmont D'Urville's (1832) division of Pacific Islanders into different races categorized by the color of their skin, and Margaret Mead's (1928) study of adolescents in Samoa growing up in a "primitive society."

The Pacific Ocean has nourished many different communities on many different islands including Aotearoa (New Zealand), so it is impossible to make general statements that apply to all of these people and places. But while the impacts of Western colonization differed all over the Pacific, colonial ideologies about race and White superiority have molded Pacific experiences all across *Moana* (the Pacific Ocean).

According to Stewart Firth (1997), the invention of "the Native" as opposed to "Europeans" is one of the most significant ideological achievements of the Western colonizer in the Pacific. This categorization allowed the *Pākehā* (the New Zealand Māori word for "New Zealand Europeans") to unite over their shared white ancestry and superiority by classifying Indigenous Pacific people as inferior based on purportedly scientific observations about race.

Being labeled "Native" rather than Pākehā had many consequences, but especially the belief in what Firth (1997) calls the "Native Mind": a characteristic that was judged and found wanting. More often than not, "Natives" have been stereotyped as weak-minded, primitive in thought, and without the ability to progress or develop beyond their rustic state without the wisdom and guidance of Pākehā colonizers.

That this stereotype has been accepted as a scientific fact can be illustrated by an article called "The Brain of the Native" published anonymously in 1938 in the *Pacific Islands Monthly* ("Pacific Islands Monthly" 1938). The author (or authors) of this article tells us that the physical construction of the "Melanesian native's brain" is markedly different from the brain of a European, and asserts that the "animal instincts of uncivilized people, which we know to be a dominating influence in the general racial character, is in reality due to an anatomical excess from which there can be no escape" (1938: 63). The claim is then made that this required a change in how the natives were educated. "At the same time, no one can deny the rapid progress in the control of animal instinct that contact with Europeans has produced in our South Sea subjects. Two generations has in many instances turned a race of cannibals into decent members of society."

It is in this context that standardized intelligence tests have been used to reinforce and perpetuate "existing structures of inequality" in Aotearoa

(Shuker 1987; Adams et al. 2005: 187). Historically, these tests have been a way to classify students and prescribe for them educational opportunities deemed appropriate to their limited abilities. In Aotearoa, the perception that Indigenous Māori were genetically unable to manage the same curriculum as Pākehā students led to the establishment of special schools where Māori students could be prepared for jobs requiring little beyond manual labor (Walker 1996). The Native Schools Act in 1867 led to an infrastructure of primary schools designated "native," and in 1941 secondary schools were added—they were all finally transferred to the general public education system in 1969 after the educational disparities were officially recognized by the publication of the Hunn Report. By that time, there were 108 such schools.

The rationale behind these native schools had impacts far beyond the shores of Aotearoa. In 1906, the New Zealand Resident Commissioner in the Cook Islands, Walter Gudgeon wrote that people there were best fitted for "the cultivation of the soil." Why so? Because "the principles of education and evolution have not yet begun to work among the Polynesians; their only idea on the subject of education is that they may thereby acquire wealth and avoid work" (Gudgeon 1906: 102). He was not only convinced of the biological inferiority of Polynesians, but also assumed they were destined to die out if they did not learn how to be industrious (Gudgeon 1906: 78). His dismissive observations were widely shared by other foreigners, and the purported lack of "civilization" in the Pacific has often been linked to colonial stereotypes of Pacific peoples as lazy, irresponsible, and untrustworthy (Firth 1997).

These negative views of Pacific people, while apparent soon after the first arrival of Europeans (for example, seen through the voyages of Captain James Cook in the late 1700s) found new support during the eugenics movement in the late nineteenth and the first half of the twentieth century. As Maile Arvin (2019) details, the Lam/Lorden interviews conducted in 1930-1931 (under the supervision of Romanzo Adams) with 206 people in Hawai'i about their attitudes towards Chinese, Hawaiians, "Chinese-Hawaiians," and "Caucasian-Hawaiians," suggest there was a widespread conviction then that out of all these, Hawaiians were the mentally most inferior.

Arvin (2019) adds further testimony to the racism popular in this period with mention of an Australian born psychologist at the University of Hawai'i, Stanley Porteus, who focused his research on testing the intelligence of what he deemed to be different races using a nonverbal test widely known as the *Porteus Maze test* (PMT). This was (and is) a set of printed mazes of varying difficulty used to evaluate the test-taker's foresight and planning abilities.

Porteus was convinced that White people were the most intelligent, and both Hawaiian and Filipino people were consistently shown to be the least intelligent (Porteus and Babcock 1926). Although his maze test is still in use, the prejudice underlying his scholarship led to protests from students at the University of Hawai'i in 1974 when Porteus was memorialized there by the naming of a building in his honor—it was only after renewed student protests in 1998 that the building was renamed Saunders Hall in 2001.

The continuing impact of the legacy of Western intelligence testing is witnessed by a paper published in Aotearoa in 1971 that proposed a new intelligence test demonstrating the racism and bias of standardized measures of intelligence testing (Archer et al. 1971). This test, called the MOTIS test (Figure 4.2), builds on common knowledge that is part of the Indigenous Māori worldview. When this test is administered, it shows that Pākehā children are not as intelligent as Māori children, thereby flipping the stereotypical assumptions often made about non-Pākehā in Aotearoa. This test makes it obvious that Pākehā children are culturally disadvantaged, and the product of homes that do not prioritize the acquisition of knowledge. Hence they are suited only for manual labor and should be educated appropriately with such lowly jobs in mind—convictions easily leading Pākehā students to internalize this negative rhetoric and feel they are inherently inferior.

Yes, this Maori version of standardized intelligence testing was satirical. It effectively underscores, however, the harm that Indigenous people have

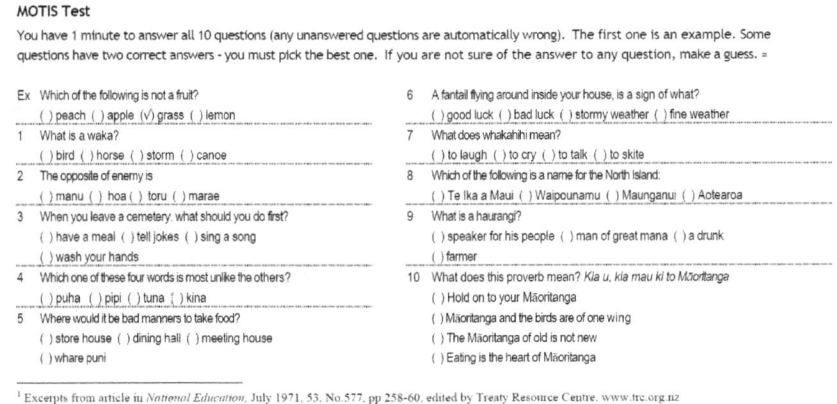

Figure 4.2. MOTIS test. Reprinted with permission, New Zealand Educational Institute.

dealt with due to the Western idea of intelligence and how it is framed around racist assumptions about knowledge as scientific and objective.

The creation of the MOTIS test was a push against Western assumptions about intelligence in 1971. Half a century since then, this foreign view of what is and isn't intelligence—and what is and isn't knowledge worthy of committing to memory—is still being used to marginalize Indigenous peoples in the Pacific. In July 2021, for example, seven academics at the University of Auckland published an open letter titled "In defense of science" asserting that *mātauranga Māori* (Māori knowledge) has no place in the science curriculum taught as part of secondary education (Clements et al. 2021). The authors claimed that Indigenous knowledge "is critical for the preservation and perpetuation of culture and local practices, and plays key roles in management and policy. However, in the discovery of empirical, universal truths, it falls far short of what we can define as science itself" (2021: 4).

This is just one example of how even current understandings of what does and doesn't constitute knowledge worth knowing are still often being based on centuries-old racist views of what it means to be intelligent. It is long past the time when these folk ideas should have been pushed into the past along with the many other harmful, racist concepts that provided the foundation (and served to excuse) colonialism in this and other parts of the world beyond Europe and North America.

What Are You Thinking About?

When we talk of intelligence, what are we thinking about? Are we all really talking about the same thing? For instance, the Oraon of Jharkhand in India say you need expertise to break earthen clods in agricultural fields using a wooden plank pulled by two oxen. A man balances on this plank to ensure that the clods of earth are evenly and carefully broken up as it is dragged through the fields. The moisture and other conditions need to be right. All of these things are taught to them by their parents from a very young age. Is this or isn't this a kind of intelligence, or at least something that can be called "know-how," or in French, *savoir-faire*?

This seemingly prosaic example shows that we need to look at intelligence through many views before we can claim to know what we are talking about. Moreover, what it means to be wise may be a judgment that depends on whether there is broad consensus about what it takes to be so. This seems particularly so when intelligence is equated with success.

Knowledge in human societies is not uniform. Being intellectually successful based on what you need to know about things and events, therefore, cannot be uniform or homogenous. Perhaps it is true that some

Figure 4.3. A *jugaad* vehicle from Gujarat called *chakda*. © Abhik Ghosh.

people are more adept at using some kinds of knowledge than others. Others may also differ in how they use what they know. Furthermore, some may keep what they know secret, and use it at their own discretion. Hence what is knowledge and what is intelligence becomes both focused and localized (Ghosh 1998).

If it is true that there is no universally acceptable definition of what is and isn't intelligence, is it at least possible to say people everywhere are willing to agree that being better than others at doing *something* using your head is important enough to single out, praise, and perhaps reward in some way such skill, such competence?

In the Hindi heartland of central India, there is a kind of cleverness that is called *jugaad*, a word literally meaning "scavenged" or "make-do." Stories about *jugaad* are legion. For example, using diesel motors or engines to power a belt repurposed to drive cycles, cycle-rickshaws, or more complex vehicles (Figure 4.3). The same word is used for transferring the engines from modern vehicles to old Willys Jeeps bought at army auctions. The resulting vehicles are then spruced up and driven with much enjoyment by the youth of Punjab in India. In fact, the term *jugaad* has become such a buzzword among the elite in India that it has often been seen as the driving force and sustaining life of the Indian economy, where making-do is the norm rather than a rare thing. Rebooting, retooling, and using old materials after repair has been stated as one of the best parts of the economy through clever (that is, intelligent) rethinking of what was available (Radjou, Prabhu, and Ahuja 2012). Years ago, the biologist

François Jacob observed that "the human brain was formed by superposition of new structures on old ones," and called this kind of inventiveness and creativity "tinkering"—adding that this was "somewhat like adding a jet engine to an old horse cart" (Jacob 1977: 1166).

What seems apparent here is that a person, or all that a person does, may not be seen as being "intelligent" in its entirety. Someone can be judged as intelligent in some ways, but how they handle other things and events may even be considered quite the opposite. In short, rarely is anyone seen as being intelligent in all ways at all times. However, there may be a widely shared consensus that some people may be more an "all-rounder" than others.

Is there something that might be called "collective intelligence?" (Shuangling et al. 2009). Those trained to be adept in a particular system of knowledge might be said to be collectively wise in this way. However, can this really be called being unusually intelligent?

Communities of practice and traditional story-telling seem to be the norm in many societies. For example, people of the Chalumna River (Xhosa: *Tyolomnqa*) estuary in the Eastern Cape Province of South Africa. Here using the resources of the estuary was guided by knowledge learnt through stories as well as through practice. Ecologically managing the estuaries was a problem which was dealt with by the community by using such methods (Mosia and Ngulube 2005).

What then does success play in judging someone to be more intelligent than others? What if someone is only successful part of the time? Does that make them come across to us as less intelligent despite their cleverness in some things? Whatever answers you favor, it seems likely that intelligence is not a constant of anyone's behavior and also changes from society to society and over the course of time.

For instance, recently a man in Jharkhand was suffering from an earache. In his desperation to get relief, he remembered something he had heard that led him to pick up insects from a stream, crush them, and then mix what he had thus extracted with oils and herbs to create an ointment that has now become a well-known remedy for earache in his neighborhood. He has also tested this ointment to find out if it still worked without including juice from these insects. It does not. Surely this kind of experimental problem solving can be labeled as intelligent, and it is valued as such in his local neighborhood.

Regardless of the answer you favor in this particular case, clearly paying attention to what is in the world around us and seeing what can be made of what we find there can have an impact on the quality of life in general and at least locally, too. We sometimes forget that housework and cooking, for example, may not strike us as signs of human brilliance, but nonetheless, they are the foundation for many "successful" ideas, practical skills, and useful—and perhaps truly brilliant—innovations.

What Does It Mean to Be Intelligent?

When we began writing this book, we thought it might be likely we would end up arguing against keeping the word *intelligence*. We have come around to the opposite conclusion. Perhaps because this is such a familiar idea, this is not a word that can be easily erased from the English language. So instead we want to redefine it.

This is easier said than done. We need to describe as clearly as we can what we think this word is often taken to mean—despite the fact, as we have noted before, this is a word that has no widely accepted dictionary or scientific definition. Then we need to say how we want to see this word redefined.

Intelligence as Decision-Making

As we have previously suggested, several characteristics are often assumed to be true about intelligence and what it is that your brain does for you:

1. It is obvious that some of us are better than others at being clever in what others would agree are critically important ways.
2. There is something called *intelligence*—a "natural ability" (Gigerenzer 2020: 597)—coded in the genes you have inherited from your parents, their parents, and your more distant ancestors that somehow biologically determines how well and how quickly you are able to meet life's challenges and opportunities.
3. Except for those who are impaired, it goes without saying that we all want to choose wisely and make the best possible decisions when we are dealing with the challenges and opportunities of life.
4. Furthermore, it is obvious that those of us who are certifiably the most intelligent should be given all the benefits and opportunities we can offer them so they may be productive and successful at what they do so abnormally well.

Although more could be said about intelligence as conventionally understood, it is common knowledge that all of us live in a world that is difficult and challenging. Even the brightest among us, therefore, cannot always know what is the right thing to do. Consequently, there is much also to be said for the idea that we are all predisposed to use basic rules of thumb that some call *heuristics* to make the job of deciding what to do (or not do) less "effortful" and time consuming. "Roughly speaking, a heuristic is a simple rule that uses a minimum of the available information . . . in order to make efficient decisions under uncertainty. The term heuristic is of Greek origin, meaning 'serving to find out or discover'" (Gigerenzer 2020: 587). The psychologist Gerd Gigerenzer has proposed, therefore, that intelligence can be understood as "the ability to find the right heuristic for a given problem" (2020: 598).

Dealing with Uncertainty

As we discussed in Chapter 2, Daniel Kahneman in *Thinking, Fast and Slow* examines in detail how easy it is for all of us to make mistakes especially when we are not taking enough time to think things through carefully. His solution? "The best we can do is a compromise: learn to recognize situations in which mistakes are likely and try harder to avoid significant mistakes when the stakes are high" (Kahneman 2011: 28). Unlike Kahneman, Gigerenzer has repeatedly argued that instead of worrying about how cautious and deliberate we are when we make decisions, what we need to know are the correct rules of thumb, the right heuristics, to deal with the problems and decisions confronting us.

Rather than taking sides with Kahneman or Gigerenzer, we want to look instead at examples of what may go wrong—or at least go poorly—when your brain is attending to what is happening outside the security of your skull. Each of the three cognitive abilities we discussed in Chapter 3 is prone to making mistakes having unintended consequences:

1. **Awareness**—Because the brain's memory traces, both situational and sequential, are impressionistic and only as detailed as your experiences have made them, what they "say." "show," or "mean" is inherently ambiguous. How ambiguous they are depends in part on how stable and predictable were the things and events that have been committed to memory (Kahneman and Klein 2009).
2. **Recognition**—The ambiguity of what you are experiencing from one moment to the next can lead the brain to "misread" and wrongly "classify" the memory traces being formed or reaffirmed by what is happening around you, or by what you are learning about the world from other people.
3. **Imagination**—Once the imaginative side of your awareness of the world has had a chance to work with the memory traces you have formed, as we said in our introduction to this book, what you make of them can be far from realistic, even quite delusional.

These are several of the reasons why it is harder to be rational than conventional wisdom might say, regardless of whether you take things slow and easy, or know the proper heuristics to use. What can be done, therefore, to counter these weaknesses in how all of us understand what is happening around us or might happen down the road?

Three Fallacies

Back when we were discussing the Salem witch trials of 1692–1693 at the start of this book, we noted that the biologist François Jacob had used the word "possible" in his short and insightful book *The Possible and the Actual* (1982) to explore how the human mind tries to decide what can or cannot be true in the real world. When you read this book, you soon realize a more truthful title would be *The Plausible, the Possible, and the Actual*, although it isn't hard to see why this might not work as a good book title. Even so, here is his explanation for why he wrote this book:

> Whether in a social group or in an individual, human life always involves a continuous dialogue between the possible and the actual. A subtle mixture of belief, knowledge, and imagination builds before us an ever changing picture of the possible. It is on this image that we mold our desires and fears. It is to this possible that we adjust our behavior and actions. In a way, such human activities as politics, art, and science can be viewed as particular ways of conducting this dialogue between the possible and the actual, each one with its own rules. (Jacob 1982: *vii–viii*).

What he makes clear here, however, is that what he has in mind isn't just a dialogue. Rather it is a trialogue. If so, then is it even possible to decide what is or isn't true in the real world? Philosophers and logicians have been trying to answer this deceptively simple question literally for thousands of years. Nonetheless, much has been written about the fallacies we need to be aware of to avoid faulty arguments and mistaken beliefs.

Awareness *and The Fallacy of Misplaced Concreteness*

The philosopher Alfred North Whitehead called it the fallacy of misplaced concreteness, "the accidental error of mistaking the abstract for the concrete" (Whitehead 1925: 72; Thompson 1997). It could also be called the fallacy of self-delusion. However labeled, this is the mistake of assuming that our impressions of the world around us are not only reliable and possibly even helpful, but also true. As Whitehead went on to observe:

"It is not necessary for the intellect to fall into the trap, though ... there has been a very general tendency to do so."

In this book, an obvious example would be intelligence. People seem shocked and evidently may not want to believe you when you tell them intelligence does not exist, cannot be measured, and is just a folk word, a conventional way of trying to explain why some of us seem to do something much better than the rest of us.

Recognition *and The Fallacy of Repetition*

Much has been written about what is called the "confirmation bias." As Raymond Nickerson remarked in 1998: "If one were to attempt to identify a single problematic aspect of human reasoning that deserves attention above all others, the confirmation bias would have to be among the candidates for consideration" (Nickerson 1998: 175). The American Psychological Association says characteristic of how we think about other people, things, and events is "the tendency to gather evidence that confirms preexisting expectations, typically by emphasizing or pursuing supporting evidence while dismissing or failing to seek contradictory evidence." B. F. Skinner simply called what is basically at the root of it all "conditioning" (see Chapter 2), which at least on the face of it sounds like a more useful label than calling it a "tendency."

Nickerson's own conclusion in 1998 was that "we seldom seem to seek evidence naturally that would show a hypothesis to be wrong and to do so because we understand this to be an effective way to show it to be right if it really is right." Nonetheless, he was seemingly optimistic that "perhaps simply being aware of the confirmation bias—of its pervasiveness and of the many guises in which it appears—might help one both to be a little cautious about making up one's mind quickly on important issues and to be somewhat more open to opinions that differ from one's own than one might otherwise be" (1998: 211).

Why do we as a species seem to have this fundamental disability? As we have discussed, one likely reason is that the repetition of an experience can strengthen how likely we are to accept something as true and correct even without our being aware of what we have experienced previously. A famous quotation often attributed to Adolph Hitler's propaganda minister Joseph Goebbels is this one: "Repeat a lie often enough and it becomes the truth."

Imagination *and The Fallacy of Categorical Causation*

Although not formally recognized by any logician we have come across, there is also another fallacy that is easy to fall prey to, one we call the fal-

Table 4.1. Three basic questions.

QUESTIONS	RELATIONAL AWARENESS
1. Can they SEE the problem?	**SURVEY**: Do you know *what* to look for?
2. Can they SOLVE the problem?	**THEORY**: Do you know *why* you should?
3. Did they CREATE the problem?	**MODEL**: Do you know *how* you could be wrong?

lacy of categorical causation. This is the belief that different things have different explanations. Examples: doing something stupid is caused by something called *stupidity*; sleep is caused by something called a *somnolent factor*; being prejudiced is caused by something called *prejudice*, and being smart is caused by something called *intelligence*.

Staying in Touch with Reality

At the end of Chapter 1, we asked you to think about how you would answer three apparently simple questions. What we did not say then is that answering these questions brings to the fore the role and importance of active awareness in dealing with the realities of the world we live in (Table 4.1).

Survey—Do You Know What *to Look For?*

Attributing success or failure in life to something as elemental and supposedly ingrained as intelligence easily ignores the shortcomings of human awareness discussed in Chapter 3. Not only are there physical and biological limitations to what we are able to perceive in the world around us, but as we discussed earlier (see page 94 here), paying attention to things and events going on around us can become harder and harder to do as we become more and more familiar with what may come across to us as the dull and boring patterning of life. What it takes to get people to be alert may need to be dramatic and widely perceived. Furthermore, much of what we know and understand about the world is only hearsay that we have acquired from others. Ironically, as we have said before, since they cannot rely on verbal communication with each other as much as we do, other animals could be ranked as more intelligent than we are.

Theory—Do You Know Why You Should?

The Polish-American philosopher Alfred Korzybski (1879–1950) famously observed almost a century ago that a map is not the territory it represents (Korzybski 1933: 58). The human brain, indeed the brain of any animal, is generally good at mapping the world as it sees, feels, and in other ways experiences it. But as Herbert Simon (see Chapter 2) insisted, what a person cannot do, he or she will not do, no matter how strong is the urge to do it. Consequently, in the face of real-world complexity, we must all be content with finding good enough answers to questions because the best answers are unknowable (Jacob 1982: 56). The most that we can be is "a satisficer, a person who accepts 'good enough' alternatives, not because less is preferred to more but because there is no choice" (Simon 1996: 28–29).

We agree with Simon, but finding "good enough" answers to life's challenges and demands calls for more than simply accepting the genuine complexity of the world we inhabit. Because of this complexity, we are all constantly being challenged from one moment to the next to decide how similar or different what we are experiencing may be from what we have previously experienced. When it isn't possible to connect the present with what we already know, we have nothing to tell us what to do next. As the popular old saying goes, "you're up the creek without a paddle."

Model—Do You Know How You Could Be Wrong?

In her commentary on the famous essays by the sixteenth-century writer Michel de Montaigne, the twentieth-century writer Virginia Woolf offers a cryptic observation: "No fact is too little to let it slip through one's fingers and besides the interest of facts themselves, there is the strange power we have of changing facts by the force of the imagination" (Woolf 1925). She is writing approvingly about Montaigne as someone "who succeeded in the hazardous enterprise of living." And yet, as she notes, his personal motto was *Que sçais-je?* (What do I know?)

Without questioning whether facts come in sizes small, medium, and large, we think juxtaposing as she does here interest in facts and the ease in which we can change facts by force of imagination hints at how our minds can delude us into thinking we know more about things and events than we do. Intelligence, if we keep this word in our dictionaries, is to be found instead in how aware we are of the likelihood that we might be wrong about what is happening and why outside the confines of our skull.

A Revealing Example

An example of how challenging it can be to figure out what is going on and why outside the confines of the skull comes from the history of medicine. It has long been known that not eating enough fruits and vegetables can make way for the deadly disease called scurvy. What wasn't always obvious is that the major cause is severe Vitamin C (ascorbic acid) deficiency.

In 1740, Commodore George Anson took command of a squadron of six ships and roughly 1,500 men sent out from Great Britain to attack Spanish possessions in South America during the War of Jenkins' Ear (1739–1748). By the time Anson returned to England in 1744, he had circumnavigated the globe via China. By then literally hundreds of his sailors had died, many from scurvy (Tröhler 2005). Yet it had been known at least since the start of the seventeenth century that a small amount of lemon juice taken daily could help prevent this from happening (Baxby 1997). It was also believed then, however, that other traditional and unproved remedies such as consuming onions, cider, or pickled cabbage could play the same role in maintaining good health. All of these are now known to have little or no Vitamin C (Armory 1997).

Ironically, even after 1795 when the British Admiralty had ordered that lemon juice be a regular part of a sailor's diet, the Admiralty was persuaded in 1848 to stop buying lemons and substitute instead limes. Limes are now known to have only about a quarter of the amount of Vitamin C. Thereafter, sailors in the British Royal Navy were required by law to drink lime juice to ward off scurvy. Sure enough, the scourge returned for the rest of that century, and it was even doubted that scurvy was a deficiency disease (Baron 1997).

This historical example documents the wisdom of the popular saying "facts matter," but also underscores how critical it is to accept the less often voiced wisdom that facts become facts when there is good reason to see them as such. This is why ideas, theories, and models matter. And why the slogan "look again" should be taken seriously.

Key Points

1. **OLD DEFINITIONS** (*Cambridge Dictionary*)
   intelligence [/ɪnˈtel.ə.dʒəns/; /ɪnˈtel.ɪ.dʒəns/] *noun* : ability to learn, understand, and make judgments or have opinions based on reason.
   intelligent [/ɪnˈtel.ə.dʒənt/; /ɪnˈtel.ɪ.dʒənt/] *adjective* : showing intelligence, or able to learn and understand things easily.

reason [/ˈriː.zən/; /ˈriː.zən/] *noun* : the cause of an event or situation or something that provides an excuse or explanation.

2. **NEW DEFINITIONS**

intelligence [/ɪnˈtel.ə.dʒəns/; /ɪnˈtel.ɪ.dʒəns/] *noun* : awareness of things, events, and changing circumstances.

intelligent [/ɪnˈtel.ə.dʒənt/; /ɪnˈtel.ɪ.dʒənt/] *adjective* : actively aware, alert, observant, attentive, insightful.

References

"Alzheimer's Disease." 2023. "Alzheimer's Disease Fact Sheet." National Institute on Aging (NIA). Downloaded on June 16, 2023. https://www.nia.nih.gov/health/alzheimers-disease-fact-sheet.

"Autism." 2023. "Autism Spectrum Disorder." U.S. National Institute of Mental Health. Downloaded on June 6, 2023. https://www.nimh.nih.gov/health/topics/autism-spectrum-disorders-asd.

"Chaos and Patterns." 2023. "Chaos and Patterns." Asia Open Source Software, 12 July. Downloaded on June 6, 2023. https://www.asia-oss.net/aossrep/patterns.htm

"Pacific Islands Monthly." 1938. "The Brain of the native (21 February 1938)." *Pacific Islands Monthly* 8(7): 63.

"PTSD." 2023. "Post-Traumatic Stress Disorder." National Institute of Mental Health. Downloaded on June 6, 2023. https://www.nimh.nih.gov/health/publications/post-traumatic-stress-disorder-ptsd

"What is truth?," Got Questions Ministries. Accessed on July 5, 2023. https://www.gotquestions.org/what-is-truth.html.

Abid, Greyson. 2022. "Recognition and the Perception–Cognition Divide." *Mind & Language* 37: 770–89. https://doi.org/10.1111/mila.12362.

Abraham, Anna, ed. 2020. *Cambridge Handbook of the Imagination*. Cambridge: Cambridge University Press. https://doi.org/10.1017/9781108580298.

Adams, Paul. 2005. "Biological Explanations of Educational Attainment." *Education and Society in Aotearoa New Zealand* (2nd ed.), Paul Adams, Roger Openshaw, and Judy Hamer, eds., 257–94. Melbourne, Australia: Thomas/Dunmore Press.

Agamben, Giorgio. 2001. *The Open: Man and Animal*. Stanford, CA: Stanford University Press. https://www.sup.org/books/title/?id=5305.

Alcoff, Linda Martín. 2007. "Mignolo's Epistemology of Coloniality." *CR: The New Centennial Review* 7: 79–101. http://www.jstor.org/stable/41949566.

Alcock, Joe, Carlo C. Maley, and C. Athena Aktipis. 2014. "Is Eating Behavior Manipulated by the Gastrointestinal Microbiota? Evolutionary Pressures and Potential Mechanisms." *Bioessays* 36: 940–49. https://doi.org/10.1002/bies.201400071.

Alexander, Robert G., Stephen L. Macknik, and Susana Martinez-Conde. 2018. "Microsaccade Characteristics in Neurological and Ophthalmic Disease." *Frontiers in Neurology* 9, article 144: 1–9. https://doi.org/10.3389%2Ffneur.2018.00144.

Allport, Gordon W. 1954. *The Nature of Prejudice*. Cambridge, MA.: Addison-Wesley Publishing Company.

Anderson, Eugene N. 1980. "'Heating' and 'Cooling' Foods in Hong Kong and Taiwan." *Social Science Information* 19: 237–68. https://doi.org/10.1177/053901848001900203.

———. 1984. "'Heating' and 'Cooling' Foods Re-examined." *Social Science Information* 23: 755–77. https://doi.org/10.1177/053901884023004006.

———. 2007. *Floating World Lost*. New Orleans: University Press of the South.

———. 2014. *Everyone Eats*, 2nd ed. New York: New York University Press.

Anderson, Eugene N., and Raymond Pierotti. 2022. *Respect and Responsibility in Pacific Coast Indigenous Nations: The World Raven Makes*. Cham, Switzerland: Springer Nature.

Archer, Dane, Roger S. Oppenheim, Timoti S. Karetu, and Ross St. George. 1971. "Intelligence and the Pakeha Child." *National Education* 53: 258–60.

Armory, David W. 1997. "Lind, Scott, Amundsen and Scurvy." *Journal of the Royal Society of Medicine* 90: 299. https://doi.org/10.1177/014107689709000527.

Aronowitz, Sara. 2019. "Memory Is a Modeling System." *Mind & Language* 34: 483–502. https://doi.org/10.1111/mila.12220.

Arvin, Maile Renee. 2019. *Possessing Polynesians: The Science of Settler Colonial Whiteness in Hawaii and Oceania*. Durham, NC and London, UK: Duke University Press.

Arzy, Shahar, and Amnon Dafni-Merom. 2020. "Imagining and Experiencing the Self on Cognitive Maps." In *Cambridge Handbook of the Imagination*, Anna Abraham, ed., 311–31. Cambridge: Cambridge University Press. https://doi.org/10.1017/9781108580298.020.

Atkinson, Richard C., and Richard M. Shiffrin. 1968. "Human Memory: A Proposed System and Its Control Processes." In *The Psychology of Learning and Motivation: Advances in Research and Theory*, Kenneth Spence and Janet Taylor Spence, eds., vol. 2, 89–195. New York: Academic Press. https://doi.org/10.1016/S0079-7421(08)60422-3.

Baddeley, Alan. 2012. "Working Memory: Theories, Models, and Controversies." *Annual Review of Psychology* 63: 1–29. https://doi.org/10.1146/annurev-psych-120710-100422.

Bandama, Foreman. 2013. The archaeology and technology of metal production in the Late Iron Age of the Southern Waterberg, Limpopo Province, South Africa. PhD dissertation, University of Cape Town.

Barker, K. Brandon, and Daniel J. Povinelli. 2019. "Conclusion: Old Ideas and the Science of Animal Folklore." *Journal of Folklore Research* 56: 113–23. https://muse.jhu.edu/article/735438.

Barker, K. Brandon. 2019. "The Animal Question as Folklore in Science." *Journal of Folklore Research* 56: 15–26. https://doi.org/10.2979/jfolkrese.56.2_3.02.

Baron, Jeremy Hugh. 1997. "Scurvy, Lancaster, Lind, Scott and Almroth Wright." *Journal of the Royal Society of Medicine* 90: 415. https://doi.org/10.1177/014107689709000726.

Baxby, Derrick. 1997. "Lind's Clinical Trial and the Control of Scurvy." *Journal of the Royal Society of Medicine* 90: 526. https://doi.org/10.1177/014107689709000926.

Berthet, Vincent., and de Gardelle Vincent. 2023. "The Heuristics-and-Biases Inventory: An Open-Source Tool to Explore Individual Differences in Rationality." *Frontiers in Psychology* 14. https://doi.org/10.3389/fpsyg.2023.1145246.

Biever, Celeste. 2023. "ChatGPT Broke the Turing Test—the Race Is on for New Ways to Assess AI." *Nature* 619: 686–89. https://doi.org/10.1038/d41586-023-02361-7.

Binda, Paola, and Maria Concetta Morrone. 2018. "Vision During Saccadic Eye Movements." *Annual Review of Vision Science* 4: 193–213. https://doi.org/10.1146/annurev-vision-091517-034317.

Blackmore, Susan. 2020. "But AST Really is Illusionism." *Cognitive Neuropsychology* 37: 206–8. https://doi.org/10.1080/02643294.2020.1729112.

Bolhuis, John J., Gillian R. Brown, Robert C. Richardson, and Kevin N. Laland. 2011. "Darwin in Mind: New Opportunities for Evolutionary Psychology." *PLoS Biology* 9(7): e1001109. https://doi.org/10.1371/journal.pbio.1001109.

Bornstein, Marc H. 2020. "Intelligence in Infancy." In *Cambridge Handbook of Intelligence*, Robert J. Sternberg, ed., 124–54. Cambridge: Cambridge University Press. https://psycnet.apa.org/doi/10.1017/9781108770422.008.

Cao Xueqin (vols. 4–5 with Gao E). 1973–1986. *The Story of the Stone*, transl. By David Hawkes and John Minford from the eighteenth-century Chinese original. New York: Penguin.

Carroll, Sean B. 2013. *Brave Genius: A Scientist, a Philosopher and Their Daring Adventures From the French Resistance to the Nobel Prize*. New York: Crown.

Chica, Ana B., Paolo Bartolomeo, and Juan Lupiáñez. 2013. "Two Cognitive and Neural Systems for Endogenous and Exogenous Spatial Attention." *Behavioural Brain Research* 237: 107–23. https://doi.org/10.1016/j.bbr.2012.09.027.

Chirikure, Shadreck. 2015. *Metals in Past Societies: A Global Perspective on Indigenous African Metallurgy*. New York: Springer.

Chomsky, Noam. 1959. "A Review of B. F. Skinner's Verbal Behavior." *Language* 35: 26–58. https://www.jstor.org/stable/411334.

———. 1971. "The Case Against B. F. Skinner." *The New York Review of Books* 17(11): 18–24.

Chu, Brianna, Komal Marwaha, Terrence Sanvictores, and Derek Ayers. 2023. "Physiology, Stress Reaction." StatPearls [Internet]. Treasure Island (FL): StatPearls Publishing. NCBI Bookshelf. A service of the National Library of Medicine, National Institutes of Health. Downloaded on May 6, 2023. https://www.ncbi.nlm.nih.gov/books/NBK541120/?report=printable.

Cieri, Filippo, Robin Lester Carhart-Harris, Christoph Mathys, Oliver Turnbull, and Mark Solms. 2023. "Editorial: Frontiers in Psychodynamic Neuroscience." *Frontiers in Human Neuroscience* 17: 1170480. https://doi.org/10.3389/fnhum.2023.1170480.

Clements, Kendall, Garth Cooper, Michael Corballis, Doug Elliffe, Robert Nola, Elizabeth Rata, and John Werry. 2021. "In Defence of Science." *New Zealand Listener*, 31 July 2021, 4. Downloaded on October 24, 2023. https://web.archive.org/web/20230610052444/https://www.fsu.nz/in_defence_of_science_article.

Cobb, Matthew. 2020. "Why Your Brain is Not a Computer." *The Guardian*, 2/27/2020. Downloaded on August 3, 2023. https://www.theguardian.com/science/2020/feb/27/why-your-brain-is-not-a-computer-neuroscience-neural-networks-consciousness?fbclid=IwAR3lW9Y8xPqpRIKXVFW6SdP0ndTrfy9ZaXK2Js08dIsqimknOm0Qoue4M9E.

Cohen, Esther. 1986. "Law, Folklore and Animal Lore." *Past & Present* 110: 6–37. https://www.jstor.org/stable/650647.

Collerton, Daniel, Elaine Perry, and Alan Robert. 2020. "Hallucinations and Imagination." In *Cambridge Handbook of the Imagination*, Anna Abraham, ed., 728–59. Cambridge: Cambridge University Press. https://doi.org/10.1017/9781108580298.044.

Colom, Roberto, Sherif Karama, Rex E. Jung, and Richard J. Haier. 2010. "Human Intelligence and Brain Networks." *Dialogues in Clinical Neuroscience* 12 489–501. https://doi.org/10.31887/DCNS.2010.12.4/rcolom.

Cosmides, Leda, and John Tooby. 1997. *Evolutionary Psychology: A Primer*. Center for Evolutionary Psychology, Santa Barbara. https://live-center-for-evolutionary-psychology.pantheonsite.io/wp-content/uploads/2023/06/Evolutionary-Psychology-A-Primer-CosmidesTooby1993.pdf.

Costandi, Moheb. 2016. *Neuroplasticity*. Cambridge, MA: MIT Press.

Crespi, Bernard J. 2020. "The Psychiatry of Imagination." In *Cambridge Handbook of the Imagination*, Anna Abraham, ed., 760–82 Cambridge: Cambridge University Press. https://doi.org/10.1017/9781108580298.045.

Daley, Christine E., and Anthony J. Onwuegbuzie. 2020. "Race and Intelligence. It's Not a Black and White Issue." In *Cambridge Handbook of Intelligence*, Robert J. Sternberg, ed., 373–94. Cambridge: Cambridge University Press. https://psycnet.apa.org/doi/10.1017/9781108770422.017.

Damassino, Nicola, and Nicholas Novelli. 2020. "Rethinking, Reworking and Revolutionising the Turing Test." *Minds and Machines* 30: 463–68. https://doi.org/10.1007/s11023-020-09553-4.

David, Nicholas, Robert Heimann, David Killick, and Michael Wayman. 1989. "Between Bloomery and Blast Furnace: Mafa Iron-smelting Technology in North Cameroon." *African Archaeological Review* 7: 183–208. https://doi.org/10.1007/BF01116843.

Davis, Katie, Joanna Christodoulou, Scott Seider, and Howard Earl Gardner. 2011. "The Theory of Multiple Intelligences." In *Cambridge Handbook of Intelligence*, Robert J. Sternberg and Scott Barry Kaufman, eds., 485–503. Cambridge: Cambridge University Press. https://doi.org/10.1017/CBO9780511977244.025.

De Boeck, Paul, Laurence Robert Gore, Trinidad González, and Ernesto San Martín. 2020. "An Alternative View on the Measurement of Intelligence and Its History." In *Cambridge Handbook of Intelligence*, Robert J. Sternberg, ed.,

47–74. Cambridge: Cambridge University Press. https://doi.org/10.1017/ 9781108770422.005.
de Neys, Wim. 2021. "On Dual and Single Process Models of Thinking." *Perspectives on Psychological Association for Psychological Science* 16: 1412–27. https:// doi.org/10.1177/1745691620964172.
Dehaene, Stanislas. 2014. *Consciousness and the Brain: Deciphering How the Brain Codes Our Thoughts*. New York: Penguin.
Dennett, Daniel. 1988. "When Philosophers Encounter Artificial Intelligence." *Daedalus* 117: 283–295. https://www.jstor.org/stable/20025148.
———. 2020. "On Solms." *Neuropsychoanalysis* 22: 51–52. https://doi.org/10.108 0/15294145.2021.1878607.
Dundes, Alan. 1971. "Folk Ideas as Units of Worldview." *Journal of American Folklore* 84: 93–103. https://doi.org/10.2307/539737.
Durkheim, Emile. 1995. *The Elementary Forms of Religious Life*, trans. Karen E. Fields (French original, 1912). New York: Free Press.
Durmont D'Urville, Jules. 1832. "Sur les iles du Grand Océan." *Bulletin de la Société de Géographie* 17: 1–21.
Eagleman, David. 2011. *Incognito: The Secret Lives of the Brain*. New York: Vintage Books.
———. 2015. *The Brain*. New York: Pantheon Books.
———. 2020. *Livewired: The Inside Story of the Ever-Changing Brain*. New York: Pantheon Books.
Epstein, Robert. 2016. "The Empty Brain." *Aeon*, 18 May 2016. Downloaded on July 15, 2022. https://aeon.co/essays/your-brain-does-not-process-informa tion-and-it-is-not-a-computer.
Evans, Jonathan St. B. T., and Keith E. Stanovich, 2013. "Dual-Process Theories of Higher Cognition: Advancing the Debate." *Perspectives on Psychological Science* 8: 223–41. https://www.jstor.org/stable/44289870.
Fanon, Frantz. 2008. *Black Skin, White Masks*, trans. Charles L. Markmann. London: Pluto. (Original work published 1952).
Felin, Teppo, Jan Koenderink, and Joachim I. Krueger. 2017. "Rationality, Perception, and the All-Seeing Eye." *Psychonomic Bulletin & Review* 24: 1040–59. https://doi.org/10.3758/s13423-016-1198-z.
Firth, Stewart. 1997. "Colonial Administration and the Invention of the Native." In *The Cambridge History of the Pacific Islanders*, Donald Denoon, Malama Meleisea, Stewart Firth, Jocelyn Linnekin, and Karen Nero, eds., 260–80. Cambridge: Cambridge University Press.
Floridi, Luciano, and Massimo Chiriatti. 2020. "GPT3: Its Nature, Scope, Limits, and Consequences." *Minds and Machines* 30: 681–94. https://doi.org/10 .1007/s11023-020-09548-1
Flynn, James R. 2007. *What Is Intelligence?: Beyond the Flynn Effect*. Cambridge: Cambridge University Press. https://psycnet.apa.org/doi/10.1017/ CBO9780511605253.
———. 2020. "Secular Changes in Intelligence: The 'Flynn Effect'." In *Cambridge Handbook of Intelligence*, Robert J. Sternberg, ed., 940–63. Cambridge: Cambridge University Press. https://doi.org/10.1017/9781108770422.040.

Flynn, Mark. 1997. "The Concept of Intelligence in Psychology as a Fallacy of Misplaced Concreteness." *Interchange* 28: 231–44. https://doi.org/10.1023/A:1007317410814.

Fonseca-Azevedo, Karina, and Suzana Herculano-Houzel. 2012. "Metabolic Constraint Imposes Tradeoff Between Body Size and Number of Brain Neurons in Human Evolution." *Proceedings of the National Academy of Sciences U.S.A.* 109 18571–18576. https://doi.org/10.1073/pnas.1206390109.

Friston, Karl. 2008. "Hierarchical Models in the Brain." *PLoS Computational Biology* 4(11): e100021. https://doi.org/10.1371/journal.pcbi.1000211.

———. 2016. "The Bayesian Savant." *Biological Psychiatry* 80: 87–89. https://doi.org/10.1016/j.biopsych.2016.05.00.

Friston, Karl J., Richard Rosch, Thomas Parr, Cathy Price, and Howard Bowman. 2017. "Deep temporal models and active inference." *Neuroscience and Biobehavioral Reviews* 77: 388–402. https://doi.org/10.1016/j.neubiorev.2017.04.009.

Geertz, Clifford. 1973. *The Interpretation of Cultures. Selected Essays by Clifford Geertz*. New York: Basic Books.

Gewirtz, Paul. 1996. "On 'I Know It When I See It.'" *Yale Law Journal* 105: 1023–47. https://doi.org/10.2307/797245.

Ghosh, Abhik. 1998. "Polarization of Knowledge Among the Oraons." *South Asian Anthropologist* 19: 79–85.

Gigerenzer, Gerd. 2007. *Gut Feelings: The Intelligence of the Unconscious*. New York: Viking.

———. 2020. "Intelligence and Decision-Making." In *Cambridge Handbook of Intelligence*, Robert J. Sternberg, ed., 580–601. Cambridge: Cambridge University Press. https://doi.org/10.1017/9781108770422.025.

Gigerenzer, Gerd, Peter M. Todd, and the ABC [Adaptive Behavior and Cognition] Research Group. 1999. *Simple Heuristics That Make Us Smart*. Oxford: Oxford University Press.

Gigerenzer, Gerd, and Wolfgang Gaissmaier. 2011. "Heuristic Decision Making." *Annual Review of Psychology* 62: 451–82. https://doi.org/10.1146/annurev-psych-120709-145346.

Gingerich, Owen. 1973. "From Copernicus to Kepler: Heliocentrism as Model and as Reality." *Proceedings of the American Philosophical Society* 117: 513–22. https://www.jstor.org/stable/986462.

———. 2004. *The Book Nobody Read: Chasing the Revolutions of Nicolaus Copernicus*. New York: Walker & Co.

Girard, Maxime, Jiamu Jiang, and Mark C. W. van Rossum. 2023. "Estimating the Energy Requirements for Long Term Memory Formation." *bioRxiv* 2023.01.16.524203. https://doi.org/10.1101/2023.01.16.524203.

Gottfredson, Linda S. 1997. "Mainstream Science on Intelligence: An Editorial with 52 Signatories, History, and Bibliography." *Intelligence* 24, 13–23. https://psycnet.apa.org/doi/10.1016/S0160-2896(97)90011-8.

Gottfredson, Linda S. 2003. "Dissecting Practical Intelligence Theory: Its Claims and Evidence." *Intelligence* 31: 343–97. https://doi.org/10.1016/S0160-2896(02)00085-5.

Graziano, Michael S.A. 2019. *Rethinking Consciousness: A Scientific Theory of Subjective Experience*. New York: W.W. Norton & Company.

———. 2020. "Consciousness and the Attention Schema: Why It Has to be Right." *Cognitive Neuropsychology* 37: 224–33. https://doi.org/10.1080/02643294.2020.1729112.

Graziano, Michael S.A., and Sabine Kastner. 2011. "Awareness as a Perceptual Model of Attention." *Cognitive Neuroscience* 2: 125–27. https://doi.org/10.1080/17588928.2011.585237.

Graziano, Michael S.A., Arvid Guterstam, Branden J. Bio, and Andrew I. Wilterson. 2019. "Toward a Standard Model of Consciousness: Reconciling the Attention Schema, Global Workspace, Higher-order Thought, and Illusionist Theories." *Cognitive Neuropsychology* 37: 155–72. https://doi.org/10.1080/02643294.2019.1670630.

Grigorenko, Elena L., and Olga Burenkova. 2020. "Genetic Bases of Intelligence." In *Cambridge Handbook of Intelligence*, Robert J. Sternberg, ed., 101–23. Cambridge: Cambridge University Press. https://doi.org/10.1017/9781108770422.007.

Grund, Peter J. 2020. "Writing the Salem Witch Trials." In *A Companion to American Literature*, vol. 1, Susan Belasco, Theresa Strouth Gaul, Linck Johnson, and Michael Soto, eds., 73–88. John Wiley & Sons. https://doi.org/10.1002/9781119056157.ch5.

Gudgeon, Walter. 2006. No 214. Cook and Other Islands Parliamentary Papers, Session II 1906, *Appendices to the Journals of the House of Representatives*, 1905, A3, page 102.

Hatfield, Gary. 2007. "The Passions of the Soul and Descartes's Machine Psychology." *Studies in the History and Philosophy of Science Part A* 38: 1–35. https://doi.org/10.1016/j.shpsa.2006.12.015.

———. 2017. "Descartes: New Thoughts on the Senses." *British Journal for the History of Philosophy* 25: 443–64. https://doi.org/10.1080/09608788.2016.1214908.

Hemmatian, Babak, and Steven A. Sloman. 2018. "Community Appeal: Explanation without Information." *Journal of Experimental Psychology: General* 147: 1677–1712. https://psycnet.apa.org/doi/10.1037/xge0000478.

Hohwy, Jakob. 2020. "New Directions in Predictive Processing." *Mind & Language* 35: 209–23. https://doi.org/10.1111/mila.12281.

Holland, Jennifer S. 2024. *Dog Smart. Life-Changing Lessons in Canine Intelligence*. Washington, D.C.: National Geographic Partners.

Holler, Simone, German Köstinger, Kevan A.C. Martin, Gregor F.P. Schuhknecht, and Ken J. Stratford. 2021. "Structure and Function of a Neocortical Synapse." *Nature* 7848: 111–16. https://doi.org/10.1038/s41586-020-03134-2.

Holyoak, Keith J., and Robert G. Morrison. 2011. "Thinking and Reasoning: A Reader's Guide." In *The Oxford Handbook of Thinking and Reasoning*, Keith J. Holyoak, and Robert G. Morrison, eds., 1–8. https://doi.org/10.1093/oxfordhb/9780199734689.013.0001.

Humphrey, Caroline with Urgunge Onon. 1996. *Shamans and Elders: Experience, Knowledge, and Power among the Daur Mongols*. Oxford: Oxford University Press.

Hunt-Grubbe, Charlotte. 2007. "The Elementary DNA of Dr Watson." *The Sunday Times*, October 14. 2007. Downloaded on October 14, 2023 from https://library.wur.nl/WebQuery/file/cogem/cogem_t49203c8e_001.pdf.

Ikäheimo, Tina M, Kari Jaakkola, Jari Jokelainen, Annaka Saukkoriipi, Merja Roivainen, Raija Juvonen, Olli Vainio, Jouni J. Jaakkola. 2016. "A Decrease in Temperature and Humidity Precedes Human Rhinovirus Infections in a Cold Climate." *Viruses* 8(9): 244. https://doi.org/10.3390/v8090244.

Jablonski, Nina G. 2021. "Skin Color and Race." *American Journal of Physical Anthropology* 175: 437–47. https://doi.org/10.1002/ajpa.24200.

Jacob, François. 1977. "Evolution and Tinkering." *Science* 196: 1161–66. https://www.science.org/doi/10.1126/science.860134.

———. 1982. *The Possible and The Actual*. New York: Pantheon Books.

Jasanoff, Alan. 2018. *The Biological Mind. How Brain, Body, and Environment Collaborate to Make Us Who We Are*. New York: Basic Books.

Jones, Parker Oiwi, Fidel Alfaro-Almagro, and Saad Jbabdi. 2018. "An Empirical, 21st Century Evaluation of Phrenology." *Cortex* 106: 26–35. https://doi.org/10.1016/j.cortex.2018.04.011.

Jung, Rex E. 2020. "A Look Back at Pioneering Theories of the Creative Brain." In *Cambridge Handbook of the Imagination*, Anna Abraham, ed., 548–62. Cambridge: Cambridge University Press. https://doi.org/10.1017/9781108580298.033.

Kahneman, Daniel. 2011. *Thinking, Fast and Slow*. New York: Farrar, Straus and Giroux.

Kahneman, Daniel, and Gary Klein. 2009. "Conditions for Intuitive Expertise: A Failure to Disagree." *American Psychologist* 64: 515–26. https://doi.org/10.1037/a0016755.

Kahneman, Daniel, and Amos Tversky. 1973. "On the Psychology of Prediction." *Psychological Review* 80: 237–51. https://psycnet.apa.org/doi/10.1037/h0034747.

Kahneman, Daniel, and Amos Tversky. 1979. "Prospect Theory: An Analysis of Decision under Risk." *Econometrica* 47: 263–92. https://doi.org/10.2307/1914185.

Kahneman, Daniel, Paul Slovic, and Amos Tversky, eds. 1982. *Judgment under Uncertainty: Heuristics and Biases*. Cambridge: Cambridge University Press.

Kandel, Eric R. 1999. "Biology and the Future of Psychoanalysis: A New Intellectual Framework for Psychiatry Revisited." *American Journal of Psychiatry* 156: 505–24. https://doi.org/10.1176/ajp.156.4.505.

Killick, David J. 2015. "Invention and Innovation in African Iron-smelting Technologies." *Cambridge Archaeological Journal* 25: 307–19. https://doi.org/10.1017/S0959774314001176.

Koch, Christof. 2019. *The Feeling of Life Itself: Why Consciousness is Widespread but Can't Be Computed*. Cambridge, MA: MIT Press.

Kornhaber, Mindy L. 2020. "The Theory of Multiple Intelligences." In *Cambridge Handbook of Intelligence*, Robert J. Sternberg, ed., 659–78. Cambridge: Cambridge University Press. https://doi.org/10.1017/9781108770422.028.

Korzybski, Alfred. 1933. *Science and Sanity: An Introduction to Non-Aristotelian Systems and General Semantics* (5th ed., 1994). Lancaster, PA: International Non-Aristotelian Library Publishing Co.

Kristjánsson, Árni, and Howard Egeth. 2019. "How Feature Integration Theory Integrated Cognitive Psychology, Neurophysiology, and Psychophysics." *Attention, Perception, & Psychophysics* 82: 7–23. https://doi.org/10.3758/s13414-019-01803-7.

Kruger, Daniel J., Maryanne L. Fisher, and Catherine Salmon. 2023. "What Do Evolutionary Researchers Believe About Human Psychology and Behavior?" *Evolution and Human Behavior* 44: 11–18. https://doi.org/10.1016/j.evolhumbehav.2022.11.002.

Kuzawa, Christopher W., Harry T. Chuganic, Lawrence I. Grossman, Leonard Lipovich, Otto Muzik, Patrick R. Hof, Derek E. Wildman, Chet C. Sherwood, William R. Leonard, and Nicholas Langek. 2014. "Metabolic Costs and Evolutionary Implications of Human Brain Development." *Proceedings of the National Academy of Sciences* 111: 13010–1301. www.pnas.org/cgi/doi/10.1073/pnas.1323099111.

Ladam, Christina, Jeffrey J. Harden, and Jason H. Windett. 2018. "Prominent Role Models: High-Profile Female Politicians and the Emergence of Women as Candidates for Public Office." *American Journal of Political Science* 62: 369–81. https://doi.org/10.1111/ajps.12351.

Legg, Shane, and Marcus Hutter. 2007a. "A Collection of Definitions of Intelligence." *Advances in Artificial General Intelligence: Concepts, Architectures and Algorithms: Proceedings of the AGI Workshop 2006*, Ben Goertzel and Pei Wang, eds., vol. 157 in *Frontiers in Artificial Intelligence and Applications*, pp. 17–24. Amsterdam, Netherlands: IOS press. https://www.calculemus.org/lect/08szt-intel/materialy/Definitions%20of%20Intelligence.html.

Legg, Shane, and Marcus Hutter. 2007b. "Universal Intelligence: A Definition of Machine Intelligence." *Minds & Machines* 17: 391–444. https://doi.org/10.1007/s11023-007-9079-x.

Leslie, Mitchell. 2000. "The Vexing Legacy of Lewis Terman." *Stanford Magazine*, July/August. https://stanfordmag.org/contents/the-vexing-legacy-of-lewis-terman

Lévi-Strauss, Claude. 1962. *La pensée sauvage*. Paris: Plon.

Lisman, John, and Eliezer J. Sternberg. 2013. "Habit and Nonhabit Systems for Unconscious and Conscious Behavior: Implications for Multitasking." *Journal of Cognitive Neuroscience* 25: 273–83. https://doi.org/10.1162/jocn_a_00319.

Liversedge, Simon P., and John M. Findlay. 2000. "Saccadic Eye Movements and Cognition." *Trends in Cognitive Sciences* 4: 6–14. https://doi.org/10.1016/s1364-6613(99)01418-7.

Lynch, Kevin. 1960. *The Image of the City*. Cambridge, MA: MIT Press.

Macpherson, Tom, Anne Churchland, Terry Sejnowski, James DiCarlo, Yukiyasu Kamitani, Hidehiko Takahashi, and Takatoshi Hikida. 2021. "Natural and Artificial Intelligence: A Brief Introduction to the Interplay Between AI and Neuroscience Research." *Neural Networks* 144: 603–13. https://doi.org/10.1016/j.neunet.2021.09.018.

Magliocco, Sabina. 2018. "Folklore and the Animal Turn." *Journal of Folklore Research* 55: 1–8. https://doi.org/10.2979/jfolkrese.55.2.01.

Marks, Jonathan. 2005. "Anthropology and The Bell Curve." In *Why America's Top Pundits Are Wrong: Anthropologist Talk Back*, Catherine Besteman and Hugh Gusterson, eds., 206–27. Berkeley: University of California Press.

Marx, Karl. 1887. *Capital. A Critique of Political Economy*, vol. 1. Moscow: Progress Publishers. https://www.marxists.org/archive/marx/works/1867-c1/ch07.htm.

Mavhunga, Clapperton Chakanetsa. 2017. "Introduction: What Do Science, Technology, and Innovation Mean from Africa? In *What Do Science, Technology and Innovation Mean from Africa?*, Clapperton Chakanetsa Mavhunga, ed., 63–78. Cambridge, MA: MIT Press.

McAdams, Tom A., Rosa Cheesman, and Yasmin I. Ahmadzadeh. 2023. "Annual Research Review: Towards a Deeper Understanding of Nature and Nurture: Combining Family-based Quasi-experimental Methods with Genomic Data." *Journal of Child Psychology and Psychiatry* 64: 693–707. https://doi.org/10.1111/jcpp.13720.

Mead, Margaret. 1928. *Coming of Age in Samoa*. New York: William Morrow.

Mercier, Hugo, and Dan Sperber. 2011. "Why Do Humans Reason? Arguments for an Argumentative Theory." *Behavioural and Brain Sciences* 34: 57–74. https://doi.org/10.1017/S0140525X10000968.

Mergenthaler, Philipp, Ute Lindauer, Gerald A. Dienel, and Andreas Meisel. 2013. "Sugar for the Brain: The Role of Glucose in Physiological and Pathological Brain Function." *Trends in Neurosciences* 36: 587–97. https://doi.org/10.1016/j.tins.2013.07.001.

Metz, Cade. 2023. "What Exactly Are the Dangers Posed by A.I.?" *New York Times*, Downloaded on October 6, 2023. https://www.nytimes.com/2023/05/01/technology/ai-problems-danger-chatgpt.html.

Mignolo, Walter D. 2007. "Delinking: The Rhetoric of Modernity, the Logic of Coloniality and the Grammar of De-Coloniality." *Cultural Studies* 21: 449–514. https://doi.org/10.1080/09502380601162647.

Millar, Boyd. 2019. "Learning to See." *Mind & Language* 35: 601–20. https://doi.org/10.1111/mila.12263.

Monod, Jacques. 1972. *Chance and Necessity. And Essay on the Natural Philosophy of Modern Biology*. New York: Vintage Books.

Morin, Alain. 2006. "Levels of Consciousness and Self-awareness: A Comparison and Integration of Various Neurocognitive Views." *Consciousness and Cognition* 15: 358–71. https://doi.org/10.1016/j.concog.2005.09.006.

Mosia, Lucky N., and Patrick Ngulube. 2005. "Managing the Collective Intelligence of Local Communities for the Sustainable Utilisation of Estuaries in the Eastern Cape, South Africa." *South African Journal of Libraries and Information Science* 71: 175–86. https://hdl.handle.net/10520/EJC61189.

Nehring, Sara M., and Benjamin C. Weiku. 2023. "Transient Global Amnesia." National Library of Medicine, National Center for Biotechnology Information. Treasure Island, FL: StatPearls Publishing. https://www.ncbi.nlm.nih.gov/books/NBK442001/.

Nettelbeck, Ted, Oliver Zwalf, and Con Stough. 2020. "Basic Processes of Intelligence." In *Cambridge Handbook of Intelligence*, Robert J. Sternberg, ed.,

471–503. Cambridge: Cambridge University Press. https://doi.org/10.1017/9781108770422.021.

Nickerson, Raymond S. 1998. "Confirmation Bias: A Ubiquitous Phenomenon in Many Guises." *Review of General Psychology* 2: 175–220. https://doi.org/10.1037/1089-2680.2.2.175.

———. 2020. "Developing Intelligence through Instruction." In *Cambridge Handbook of Intelligence*, Robert J. Sternberg, ed., 205–37. Cambridge: Cambridge University Press. https://doi.org/10.1017/9781108770422.011.

Oberauer, Klaus. 2019. "Working Memory and Attention–A Conceptual Analysis and Review." *Journal of Cognition* 2: 36, 1–23. https://doi.org/10.5334/joc.58.

Overskeid, Geir. 2007. "Looking for Skinner and finding Freud." *American Psychologist* 62: 590–95. https://psycnet.apa.org/doi/10.1037/0003-066X.62.6.590.

Parkinson, C. Northcote. 1955. "Parkinson's Law." *The Economist*, 19 November 1955, 177: 635–637. Downloaded on July 14, 2023. https://www.economist.com/news/1955/11/19/parkinsons-law.

Pi, Youguo, Wenzhi Liao, Mingyou Liu, and Jianping Lu. 2008. In *Pattern Recognition Techniques, Technology and Applications*, Yin, Peng-Yeng, ed., pages 433–62. *InTechOpen*. I-Tech, Vienna, Austria. https://doi.org/10.5772/6251.

Pinker, Steven. 2002. *The Blank Slate: The Modern Denial of Human Nature*. New York: Viking.

Poletti, Martina, and Michele Rucci. 2016. "A Compact Field Guide to the Study of Microsaccades: Challenges and Functions." *Vision Research* 118: 83–97. https://doi.org/10.1016/j.visres.2015.01.018.

Porteus, Stanley D., and Marjorie Elizabeth Babcock. 1926. *Temperament and Race*. Boston, MA: Richard G. Badger.

Pulvermüller, Friedemann. 2023. "Neurobiological Mechanisms for Language, Symbols and Concepts: Clues from Brain-constrained Deep Neural Networks." *Progress in Neurobiology* 230: 102511. https://doi.org/10.1016/j.pneurobio.2023.102511.

Radjou, Navi, Jaideep Prabhu, and Simone Ahuja. 2012. *Jugaad Innovation: Think Frugal, Be Flexible, Generate Breakthrough Growth*. Hoboken, NJ: John Wiley & Sons.

Ramachandran, Vilayanur Subramanian 2011. *The Tell-Tale Brain: A Neuroscientist's Quest for What Makes Us Human*. New York: W.W. Norton & Company.

Râmakrishna. 1907. *The Gospel of Râmakrishna*. New York: The Vedanta Society. Downloaded on July 18, 2020. https://books.google.com/books?id=JFEMAAAAYAAJ&pg=PR3#v=onepage&q&f=false.

Reis, Sally M., and Joseph S. Renzulli, J. 2020. "Intellectual Giftedness." In *Cambridge Handbook of Intelligence*, Robert J. Sternberg, ed., 291–316. Cambridge: Cambridge University Press. https://doi.org/10.1017/9781108770422.014.

Reisner, Steven. 1999. "The Scientific Status of Unconscious Processes: Is Freud Really Dead?" *Journal of the American Psychoanalytic Association* 47: 1061–106. https://doi.org/10.1177/00030651990470404.

Richardson, Ken. 2012. "Heritability Lost; Intelligence Found." *EMBO Reports* 13: 591–95. https://doi.org/10.1038/embor.2012.83.

Ropper, Allan H. 2023. "Transient Global Amnesia." *New England Journal of Medicine* 388: 635–40. https://doi.org/10.1056/nejmra2213867.

Rosen, Steven. 2009. "Should Scientists Study Race and IQ? NO: Science and Society Do Not Benefit." *Nature* 457: 786–88. https://doi.org/10.1038/457786a.

Satel, Sally, and Scott O. Lilienfeld. 2014. *Brainwashed. The Seductive Appeal of Mindless Neuroscience.* New York: Basic Books.

Seger, Carol A., and Earl K. Miller. 2010. "Category Learning in the Brain." *Annual Review of Neuroscience* 33: 203–19. https://doi.org/10.1146/annurev.neuro.051508.135546.

Seth, Anil. 2021. *Being You: The New Science of Consciousness.* New York: Penguin.

Seth, Anil K., and Tim Bayne. 2022. "Theories of Consciousness." *Nature Reviews Neuroscience* 23, 439–52. https://doi.org/10.1038/s41583-022-00587-4.

Shuangling, Luo, Haoxiang Xia, Taketoshi Yoshida, and Zhongtuo Wang. 2009. "Toward Collective Intelligence of Online Communities: A Primitive Conceptual Model." Journal of Systems Science and Systems Engineering 18: 203–21. https:/doi.org/10.1007/s11518-009-5095-0.

Shuker, Roy. 1987. *The One Best System? A Revisionist History of State Schooling in New Zealand.* Palmerston North, N.Z.: Dunmore Press.

Simon, Herbert A. 1956. "Rational Choice and the Structure of the Environment." *Psychological Review* 63: 129–38. https://psycnet.apa.org/doi/10.1037/h0042769.

———. 1978. "Rationality as Process and as Product of Thought." *American Economic Review* 68: 1–16. https://www.jstor.org/stable/1816653.

———. 1980. "The Behavioral and Social Sciences." *Science* 209: 72–78. https://doi.org/10.1126/science.7025205.

———. 1996. *Sciences of the Artificial*, 3rd ed. Cambridge, MA: M.I.T. Press.

Simonton, Dean Keith. 2021. "Giftedness, Talent, and Genius: Untangling Conceptual Confusions." In *Conceptions of Giftedness and Talent*, Robert J. Sternberg and Don Ambrose, eds., 393–406. Palgrave Macmillan. https://doi.10.1007/978-3-030-56869-6_22.

Skinner, Burrhus Frederic. 1953. *Science and Human Behavior.* New York: Macmillan.

———. 1971. *Beyond Freedom and Dignity.* New York: Alfred A. Knopf.

———. 1977. "Why I Am Not a Cognitive Psychologist." *Behaviorism* 5: 1–10. https://www.jstor.org/stable/27758892.

———. 1981. "Selection by Consequences." *Science* 213: 501–4. https://doi.org/10.1126/science.7244649.

———. 1990. "Can Psychology Be a Science of Mind?" *American Psychologist* 45: 1206–10. https://psycnet.apa.org/doi/10.1037/0003-066X.45.11.1206

Smith, Subrena E. 2020. "Is Evolutionary Psychology Possible?" *Biological Theory* 15: 39–49. https://doi.org/10.1007/s13752-019-00336-4.

Stanovich, Keith E., Maggie E. Toplak, and Richard F. West. 2020. "Intelligence and Rationality." In *Cambridge Handbook of Intelligence*, Robert J. Sternberg, ed., 1106–39. Cambridge: Cambridge University Press. https://doi.org/10.1017/9781108770422.047.

Sternberg, Eliezer J. 2015. *NeuroLogic: The Brain's Hidden Rationale Behind Our Irrational Behavior*. New York: Vintage Books.

Sternberg, Robert J. 1984. "Toward a Triarchic Theory of Human Intelligence." *Behavioral and Brain Sciences* 7: 269–315. https://doi.org/10.1017/S0140525X00044629.

———. 1999. "Successful Intelligence: Finding a Balance." *Trends in Cognitive Sciences* 3: 436–442. https://doi.org/10.1016/S1364-6613(99)01391-1.

———. 2005. "Intelligence." In *Cambridge Handbook of Thinking and Reasoning*, Keith J. Holyoak and Robert G. Morrison, eds., 751–73. Cambridge: Cambridge University Press.

———. 2020a. "The Augmented Theory of Successful Intelligence." In *Cambridge Handbook of Intelligence*, Robert Sternberg, ed., 679–708. Cambridge: Cambridge University Press. https://doi.org/10.1017/9781108770422.029.

———. 2020b. "The Concept of Intelligence." In *Cambridge Handbook of Intelligence*, Robert J. Sternberg, ed., 3–17. Cambridge: Cambridge University Press. https://doi.org/10.1017/9781108770422.002.

———. 2020c. "A History of Research on Intelligence: Part 1: Pre–Twentieth-Century Origins in Philosophy." In *Cambridge Handbook of Intelligence*, Robert J. Sternberg, ed., 18–30. Cambridge: Cambridge University Press. https://doi.org/10.1017/9781108770422.003.

Stetka, Bret, and Bomboland. 2019. "Mind Over Meal." *Scientific American* 320: 46–51. https://www.jstor.org/stable/10.2307/27265034.

Stoneman, Betty J. 2023. "Sartre's Imaginary and the Problem of Whiteness." *Philosophy & Social Criticism* 49: 3–17. https://doi.org/10.1177/01914537211017582.

Sundet, Jon Martin, Dag G. Barlaug, and Tore M. Torjussen. 2004. "The End of the Flynn Effect?: A Study of Secular Trends in Mean Intelligence Test Scores of Norwegian Conscripts During Half a Century." *Intelligence* 32: 349–62. https://doi.org/10.1016/j.intell.2004.06.004.

Terman, Lewis M. 1917. "Binet Scale and the Diagnosis of Feeble-Minded." *Journal of Criminal Law and Criminology* 7: 530–43. https://www.jstor.org/stable/1133997.

Terrell, John Edward. 2014. *A Talent for Friendship: Rediscovery of a Remarkable Trait*. New York: Oxford University Press.

Terrell, John Edward, and Gabriel Stowe Terrell. 2020. *Understanding the Human Mind. Why You Shouldn't Trust What Your Brain Is Telling You*. New York and London: Routledge.

Thompson, H. Edward, III. 1997. "The Fallacy of Misplaced Concreteness: Its Importance for Critical and Creative Inquiry." *Interchange* 28: 219–30. https://doi.org/10.1023/A:1007313324927.

Tigner, Robert B., and Steven S. Tigner. 2000. "Triarchic Theories of Intelligence: Aristotle and Sternberg." *History of Psychology* 3: 168–76. https://doi.org/10.1037/1093-4510.3.2.168.

Tröhler, Ulrich. 2005. "Lind and Scurvy: 1747 to 1795." *Journal of the Royal Society of Medicine* 98: 519–22. https://doi.org/10.1177/014107680509801120.

Tully, Tim. 2003. "Pavlov's Dogs." *Current Biology* 13: PR117-R119. https://doi.org/10.1016/S0960-9822(03)00066-6.

Turing, Alan M. 1950. "Computing Machinery and Intelligence." *Mind* 59: 433–60. https://www.jstor.org/stable/2251299. Also available at https://psycnet.apa.org/doi/10.1093/mind/LIX.236.433.

van Ede, Freek, and Anna C. Nobre. 2023. "Turning Attention Inside Out: How Working Memory Serves Behavior." *Annual Review of Psychology* 74: 137–65. https://doi.org/10.1146/annurev-psych-021422-041757.

van Rossum, Mark C.W. 2023. "Competitive Plasticity to Reduce the Energetic Costs of Learning." *bioRxiv* 2023.04.04.535544. https://doi.org/10.1101/2023.04.04.535544.

Verplanken, Bas, and Sheina Orbell. 2022. "Attitudes, Habits, and Behavior Change." *Annual Review of Psychology* 73: 327–52. https://doi.org/10.1146/annurev-psych-020821-011744.

Walker, Ranginui. 1996. *Ngā Pepa a Ranginui. The Walker Papers*. Auckland, New Zealand: Penguin Books.

Wallace, Anthony F. C. 1961. "The Psychic Unity of Human Groups." In *Studying Personality Cross-Culturally*, Bert Kaplan, ed., 129–64. New York. Evanston, Ill., and Elmsford, NY: Harper & Row, Publishers.

Walrath, Robert, John O. Willis, Ron Dumont, and Alan S. Kaufman. 2020. "Factor-Analytic Models of Intelligence." In *Cambridge Handbook of Intelligence*, Robert J. Sternberg, ed., 75–98. https://doi.org/10.1017/9781108770422.006.

Weinberger, Joel, and Valentina Stoycheva. 2020. *The Unconscious: Theory, Research, and Clinical Implications*. New York: Guilford Publications.

Weisswange, Thomas H., Constantin. A. Rothkopf, Todias Rodemann, and Jochen Triesch. 2009. "Can Reinforcement Learning Explain the Development of Causal Inference in Multisensory Integration?" 2009 IEEE 8th International Conference on Development and Learning, Shanghai, China, 2009, pp. 1–7. https://doi.org/10.1109/DEVLRN.2009.5175531.

Weston, Drew. 1999. "The Scientific Status of Unconscious Processes: Is Freud Really Dead?" *Journal of the American Psychoanalytic Association* 47: 1061–106. https://doi.org/10.1177/000306519904700404.

White, Gabrielle D. V. 2013. "Should We Take Kant Literally?: On Alleged Racism in *Observations on the Feeling of the Beautiful and Sublime*." *Philosophy and Literature* 37: 542–53. https://doi.org/10.1353/phl.2013.0028.

Whitehead, Alfred North. 1925. *Science and the Modern World. Lowell Lectures, 1925*. New York: The Macmillan Company. https://www.gutenberg.org/ebooks/68611.

Wilterson, Andrew I., and Michael S. A. Graziano. 2021. "The Attention Schema Theory in a Neural Network Agent: Controlling Visuospatial Attention Using a Descriptive Model of Attention." *Proceedings of the National Academy of Sciences* 118, no. 33: e2102421118. https://doi.org/10.1073/pnas.2102421118.

Wood, Wendy, and Dennis Rünger. 2016. "Psychology of Habit." *Annual Review of Psychology* 67: 289–314. https://doi.org/10.1146/annurev-psych-122414-033417.

Woodworth, Robert S., and Harold Schlosberg. 1954. *Experimental Psychology*, rev. ed. New York: Holt, Rinehart and Winston.

Woolf, Virginia. 1925. *The Common Reader*. New York: Harcourt, Brace and Company. Downloaded on May 3, 2023. https://www.gutenberg.org/cache/epub/64457/pg64457-images.html#The_Common_Reader.

Xie, Weizhen, and Weiwei Zhang. 2022cres. "Pre-existing Long-term Memory Facilitates the Formation of Visual Short-term Memory." In *Visual Memory*, Timothy F. Brady and Wilma A. Bainbridge, 84–104. Routledge. https://doi.org/10.4324/9781003158134.

Zentall, Thomas R. 2020. "Animal Intelligence." In *Cambridge Handbook of Intelligence*, Robert J. Sternberg, ed., 397–427. Cambridge: Cambridge University Press. https://psycnet.apa.org/doi/10.1017/9781108770422.018.

Zheng, Jie, Andrea G. P. Schjetnan, Mar Yebra, Bernard A. Gomes, Clayton P. Mosher, Suneil K. Kalia, Taufik A. Valiante, Adam N. Mamelak, Gabriel Kreiman, and Ueli Rutishauser. 2022. "Neurons Detect Cognitive Boundaries to Structure Episodic Memories in Humans." *Nature Neuroscience* 25: 358–68. https://doi.org/10.1038/s41593-022-01020-w.

Zittoun, Tania, Vlad Glăveanu, and Hana Hawlina. 2020. "A Sociocultural Perspective on Imagination" In *Cambridge Handbook of the Imagination*, Anna Abraham, ed., 143–61. Cambridge: Cambridge University Press. https://doi.org/10.1017/9781108580298.010.

Zlomuzica, Armin, and Ekrem Dere. 2022. "Towards an Animal Model of Consciousness Based on the Platform Theory." *Behavioural Brain Research* 419: 113695. https://doi.org/10.1016/j.bbr.2021.113695.

INDEX

African science, 8–11
agency, 25, 43, 69
Alzheimer's disease, 95–96, 97
artificial intelligence (AI), 12, 18, 62, 67, 84
astronomy, 4–5
autism spectrum disorder (ASD), 96, 97
awareness, 18, 20, 64–72, 79, 86–88, 91, 95
  mechanical, 20, 25, 54, 59, 88–89, 92, 95
  functional, 20, 89, 92, 97–98
  relational, 20, 89–90, 92, 97–98
  summary, 71–72

behaviorism. *See* Skinner, B. F.
Blind Men and the Elephant, parable, 44–45
bloomery technology, 10
bounded rationality, 50–51
brain, human
  a camera, 13, 16, 70
  a computer, 13–14, 62, 69
  a pattern recognition device, 14, 15–16, 49, 55, 75–80, 83, 89–90, 91, 111

Cartesian graphs, 23–24, 26
categories, categorical thinking, 1–2, 23–24, 26–27, 78–80, 99, 101, 110–11
chakda (a vehicle). *See jugaad*, 105
Chance and Necessity (*Le Hasard et la Nécessité*, book by Jacques Monod), 42–42
classification, 78–80, 98

Cohen, Esther, 28–30
colds, catching, 7–8
colonialism, 8–11, 100–4
confirmation bias, 110
conspiracy theories, 7
Copernicus, Nicholas, 4, 67
Crespi, Bernard, 81
cultural symbols, 48–49, 55

Darwin, Charles, 47, 51
delusion, delusional, 18–19, 39, 59, 69, 84, 85, 88, 108, 109
Descartes, René, 30–31, 61–62
Dundes, Alan, 98–99

Eagleman, David, 16–18, 76, 94
environment, 8, 32–34, 35, 39, 45, 48, 50–51, 54–55, 76, 86–88, 94
environmentalism. *See* Skinner, B. F.
Epstein, Robert, 13–14
eugenics, 30, 36, 100, 102
evolution, evolutionary theory, 23, 26, 33–34, 42, 45, 47, 51, 60, 94. 95, 102

fallacies, 109–11
folk ideas, folklore, 1, 28, 29–30, 82, 84, 98–99, 100, 104, 110
Freud, Sigmund, 31–32, 46, 66, 95

Geertz, Clifford, 45, 48–49, 55–56
genes, genetics, 9, 32–34, 37, 42–44, 49, 58, 88, 92, 94, 107
genius, 1, 12, 35
giftedness, 32–33
Gigerenzer, Gerd, 54, 90, 108

Graziano, Michael, 79

heuristics, heuristic strategies 3, 52, 54, 72, 79, 90. 108–9

imagination, 81–85, 91, 95, 96–97
   summary, 84
India, local understandings of intelligence, 104–7
intelligence
   about success, 14–15, 39, 45, 50, 56, 57, 58, 72, 86–87, 101, 104, 106–7, 111
   definitions, 1–3, 11–13, 15, 19–20, 21–23, 25, 27, 37, 39, 43, 51, 57, 62, 64–65, 81, 85–87, 105, 107, 111, 113–14
   limitations, 16–18, 50–51, 54, 60, 68, 71, 111
   measurement, 1–2, 12, 21–23, 32, 35–37, 40, 62–64, 81, 85–86, 88, 103, 110
IQ (intelligence quotient), xv, 32, 35–37, 40, 64, 71, 88, 93, 100
intuition, 15–16, 52–53, 54, 57, 90
intuitive perception, 15, 25, 88, 90–91

Jacob, François, 7, 34, 58, 77, 106, 109, 112. *See also The Possible and the Actual*
Jung, Rex, 81
jugaad (a word meaning scavenged or make-do), 105–6

Kahneman, Daniel, 45, 52–54, 56, 57, 58, 64, 72, 79, 94, 108. *See also Thinking, Fast and Slow*
Kandel, Eric, 31
key points, 20, 40, 58, 91, 113
Korzybski, Alfred, 112

Linnaeus, Carl, 2, 3, 64
logic, logicians, 25, 37, 41–42, 43, 50, 66, 71, 78, 80, 86, 109, 110

Marks, Jonathan, 35, 36
memory, memories, 13–14, 16, 18, 19, 21, 48, 51, 57, 63, 69–84, 89–90, 94, 96, 98, 104, 108
metallurgy, technology of, 10–11
Monod, Jacques, 42–43. *See also Chance and Necessity*

Montaigne, Michel de, 112
MOTIS Test (Māori intelligence test), 103–4

nature vs. nurture, 33–34, 41, 43, 44, 49, 54, 57, 58, 88, 92, 94
neuroscience, 18, 31–32, 62–63, 69, 79

Pacific Islanders, colonialism and discrimination, 100–4
pattern recognition, 15, 78–80, 89, 91
Pavlov, Ivan, 41, 47
Parkinson's Law, 92–93
phlogiston, 37–38, 39
The Possible and the Actual (book by François Jacob), 7, 109
post-traumatic stress disorder (PTSD), 96, 97

racism, 8–11, 102–3
Ramachandran, V. S., 88
rational, rationality, 1–2, 12, 15, 30, 41, 44, 50–51, 54, 56–57, 61, 66, 85, 93, 109
reason, reasoning, 2, 3, 11, 12, 27, 37, 41, 43, 48, 52, 57, 58, 62, 64–65, 66, 94, 110, 113, 114
recognition, 72–80, 91, 95, 96
   summary, 80
relational thinking, 20, 25, 26–27, 88–90, 92, 97–98, 111

Salem Witch Trials, 4, 6–7, 109
saltimbocca, 3, 85, 93
scurvy, Vitamin C deficiency, 113
schema theory, 79
Science and Human Behavior (book by B. F. Skinner), 46
The Sciences of the Artificial (book by Herbert Simon), 51
sequential mapping, 16–17, 77, 89, 108
six questions + 1, 26, 49
Simon, Herbert, 15, 45, 50–51, 55–56, 57, 79, 93, 112. *See also The Science of the Artificial*
situational mapping, 16–17, 77, 89, 108
Skinner, B. F., 45–48, 49, 50, 51, 55–56, 66, 72, 79, 85, 89, 110. *See also Science and Human Behavior*
Sleeping dogs, allegory, 60–61
Stanovich, Keith, 15, 57

Sternberg, Robert, 14–15, 19, 21–23, 28, 64, 83, 86–87, 95

Te Moana-nui-a-kiwa (Māori for "Pacific Ocean"), 100–4
Terman, Louis, 35–36, 100
ternary plots, ternary graphs, triangle plots, 24–25, 26, 43, 74, 94–95
   examples, 24, 27, 43, 56, 65, 98
Thinking
   lazy, 45, 54, 57, 94
   System 1, Type 1, 52–54
   System 2, Type 2, 53–54
Thinking, Fast and Slow (book by Daniel Kahneman), 52–54, 108
Troxler effect, 94
truth, 11–12, 44, 46, 94, 100, 104, 110

universe, models of, 4, 5

Wechsler Adult Intelligence Scale (WAIS), xiv
Whitehead, Alfred North, 109
Woolf, Virginia, 112

www.ingramcontent.com/pod-product-compliance
Lightning Source LLC
Chambersburg PA
CBHW071715020426
42333CB00017B/2278